# Praise for
# *The Gospel for Enthusiasts*

"Jeff and I are thankful the Lord has provided more gospel-centered Enneagram teachers like Tyler Zach. Whether you are new to the Enneagram or have studied it for years, we know that you'll find lasting value in this book. On these pages, Tyler's creative wisdom shines, and his focus always remains on Jesus."

— Beth & Jeff McCord, co-founders of Your Enneagram Coach, best-selling authors of *Becoming Us: Using the Enneagram to Create a Thriving Gospel-Centered Marriage*

"Tyler skillfully weaves the perfect blend of biblical wisdom and Enneagram knowledge in such an engaging and personal way. I don't know how he does it—but it feels like he wrote this book exclusively for me! His stories, examples, quotes, and Bible verses are so expertly selected and presented in such a relevant and helpful way—encouraging me to grow in sanctification and self-awareness."

— Ben Lueders, founder of Fruitful Design & Strategy and host of the *Growing a Fruitful Brand* podcast

"Tyler's sensitively woven book handles the delicate and often deeply hidden inner chambers of a Seven's heart with both a sense of fun, gentle clarity, and wisdom, beckoning Sevens to plunge into God's truest purpose for them. In these refreshing pages, eager Sevens will find both what true freedom means as well as the surprising blessing found in the depths of a life anchored by Christ. These devotions bring Sevens an invitation they desperately need: to exchange their frenetic pacing and weary hearts for still waters and lighter burdens as they release their fears to God."

— Christa Hardin, author and host of the *Enneagram & Marriage* podcast

"I have been eagerly waiting for Tyler Zach's new book on my type. This devotional is compelling and beyond profound. It's wonderful to see the Word of God come alive and apply the gospel uniquely to me!"

— John Fooshee, pastor and president of People Launching and Gospel Enneagram

"I love the way Tyler holds space in this book for the Enthusiasts to be who they are. He shares funny stories, brings the gospel into the big picture, and provides space for them to journal and self-reflect as they seek to grow in their relationship with God."

— Jackie Brewster, best-selling author of *Hearing God Speak: A 52-Week Interactive Enneagram Devotional*

"Tyler's insightful and transformative words on Enneagram Type 7 are a must-read for all enthusiasts seeking to embrace their unique strengths and live a more fulfilling life. His compassionate approach empowers 7s to honor their God-given gifts while providing actionable steps for personal growth. This book is more than faux freedom for 7s; it is liberating for 7s in amazing ways."

— Milton Stewart, host of *Do It For The Gram: An Enneagram Podcast*

"As a Type 7, I crave variety and entertainment, and Tyler's devotional delivers precisely that. Tyler skillfully intertwines Enneagram wisdom with the timeless truths of the gospel, providing fellow Type 7s a pathway to liberate themselves from the constraints of our personality box. With each chapter, you can delve into the depths of your desires and fears (with a generous side of humor), alongside insightful reflections and thought-provoking prompts."

— Amy Wicks, author and host of the Simply Wholehearted podcast

"As a 7 who's spent my entire life seeking joy, I've cried out with the Preacher of Ecclesiastes that it is all chasing after mist. Joy seems so fleeting. If you find yourself as a joy-addict and yet unsatisfied, I highly commend you Zach's book, which will point you to the only One who promises eternal joy."

— Sean Nolan, pastor of Engage Albany

"This book led me on an adventure! It was dynamic, enjoyable, and resonated deeply within me."

— Austin Edwards, pastor of Citylight Lincoln

# The Gospel for Enthusiasts

A 40-Day Devotional for
Fun, Optimistic Adventurers

BY TYLER ZACH

*To Demarick, who discipled me out of shame and into grace,*

*and all my other Enthusiast friends, whose relentless pursuit*

*of joy, unwavering optimism, and ability to find light in*

*even the darkest moments, continue to inspire me!*

# Table of Contents

WHEN JEFF AND I FIRST DISCOVERED THE Enneagram, it wasn't easy finding books written from a Christian worldview. We understood how important gospel-centered Enneagram resources could be, and that inspired us to start our business, Your Enneagram Coach. Since then, we've helped over one million people find their Type through our free assessment and grow through our online classes, coaching certifications, books, and podcast.

Type Sevens are joyful, enthusiastic, and social people who radiate optimism. As lovers of variety, they live life big and are eager to enjoy all the new experiences this world offers. They see endless possibilities and innovation all around them. Having benefited from having Type Sevens on my team, I know firsthand the joy, positivity, and exceptional creative achievements Type Sevens bring to every situation.

The Enneagram is a tool that clarifies our fallen nature while also reminding us that we are created in the *imago Dei* (image of God). When Jeff and I understood the why behind our thoughts and actions, it transformed how we looked at ourselves, our relationship with God, our marriage, our parenting, and (obviously) our careers. Taking a risk by starting a business was both exciting and terrifying. We could have easily spun out of control or run out of gas (at times, we did!), but knowing the Enneagram, as seen through the lens of the gospel, kept us grounded and on track.

The world needs Type Sevens because you uniquely bless others with your exciting insights and creative solutions, and you are always willing to try something new. Like Christ, you give others hope for the future by envisioning the many possibilities life has to offer. You inspire others to pursue their dreams and overcome their obstacles.

Like all numbers, Type Sevens experience seasons of struggle. To you, life is like cotton candy—it's super sweet to the taste, but it disappears quickly, and you're constantly unsatisfied. When life is hard, you quickly escape to things that please you to avoid the painful feelings you fear. A gospel-centered Enneagram can help you find true contentment in Christ's fountain of living water, which never runs dry. Type Sevens, this 40-day devotional will guide you to the satisfaction you desire so you can be truly present in life and with others.

Jeff and I are thankful the Lord has provided more gospel-centered Enneagram teachers like Tyler Zach. Whether you are new to the Enneagram or have studied it for years, we know you'll find lasting value in this book. On these pages, Tyler's creative wisdom shines, and his focus always remains on Jesus. We're praying God will meet you on these pages, and you will recognize your inherent value as His beloved child.

Jesus is the author and perfecter of our faith (Hebrews 12:2). He finished the great task He set out to accomplish (John 19:30). A vital part of His ministry was to stay in alignment with His Father, and He did this by setting aside time for rest and reflection. He invites you to do the same—to come away, to separate from the crowds and be with him. Remember, you are loved and valued for simply being you. You do not have to gain Christ's approval. You are accepted right now as you are.

**—Beth and Jeff McCord**
co-founders of Your Enneagram Coach
best-selling authors of *Becoming Us: Using the Enneagram to Create a Thriving Gospel-Centered Marriage*

# The Gospel for Enthusiasts

WE ARE GOING TO HAVE A LOT OF FUN! This is not going to be another boring devotional. Just look at the cover! I carefully chose the color orange, which represents optimism, creativity, appetite, and adventure, to give you a taste of what's inside. I hope all of these descriptors become hashtags you use when sharing this book!

I have a bias toward Type Seven Enthusiasts. It's not intentional. It's just that most of my best friends are Sevens. I love that you take Jesus seriously but not yourself. I love that you don't get embarrassed but laugh when you fall down a ski slope or awkwardly sing karaoke, and I love that you listen to and genuinely enjoy Top 40 music! I love that we can exchange jokes that are borderline inappropriate. Life is just so much better with you; even when the storm clouds gather, you show us that we can still dance in the rain.

I know it can feel like an uphill battle sometimes worshiping next to Pharisee Phil on Sundays or working next to Negative Nancy on Mondays. That's why I wrote this book—to be an encouraging friend offering an abundance of support as you navigate the mentally taxing and sometimes overwhelming negativity that exists in our world. Everyone knows you are assertive and thick-skinned, but what they might not see is the very tender heart underneath longing to be nurtured and courageously cheered on.

Over the next 40 days, I want to come alongside to help you become a *resident*, not a *tourist*, in the "promised land" God has given you. Being a tourist is fun, with many opportunities to sightsee and perhaps even go on a food tour, tasting some exquisite milk and honey. But a resident gets to form a deeper connection with the land, build long-term relationships, experience safety and stability, and receive a lifetime access to, well, milk and honey. However, the price of becoming a resident is courage. There are giants in the land that must be driven out. For Sevens, one giant in particular will make you want to take the long way around the promised land: *pain.* Like Joshua in the Bible, you too must resist the voices telling you to settle for the short-lived pleasures of being a tourist. Instead, fight, face your pain giant, and inherit the abundant life God has for you. *More* waits for you if you decide right now that you'll go through the pain rather than around it.

## What Makes This Book Different?

While other books explain the Enneagram, this book's primary aim is to go deeper by applying the truth of God's Word specifically to your type over the next 40 days. If you are suspicious of the Enneagram or know someone who is, download my free resource called *Should Christians Use the Enneagram?* at gospelforenneagram.com. I pray it will help you engage with this system as a Christian and then talk about it with others.

Before we get to the daily devotions, let's look at how the gospel both affirms and challenges the unique characteristics of your type.

## The Gospel Affirms Enthusiasts

God sympathizes with the worldview of an Enthusiast. This negative world lacks joy in many ways and is filled with dull, serious, and rigid people. We need positive, energetic enthusiasts who will lift our spirits when we are hurting, help us see the silver lining when we are held captive by life's circumstances, teach us how to create a fun and life-giving culture, and cast vision for us to take advantage of new opportunities rather than play it safe. Therefore, an Enthusiast will be happy to know the Bible affirms the following beliefs:

• **God created us for joy and pleasure.** "You make known to me the path of life; in your presence, there is fullness of joy; at your right hand are pleasures forevermore."[1]

---

1   Psalm 16:11

- **God created us to be joyful every day.** "Rejoice always, pray without ceasing, give thanks in all circumstances; for this is the will of God in Christ Jesus for you."[2]

- **God created us to express our enthusiasm.** "Clap your hands, all peoples! Shout to God with loud songs of joy!"[3]

- **God created us to be satisfied.** "For he satisfies the longing soul, and the hungry soul he fills with good things."[4]

- **God created us to be free**. "For freedom Christ has set us free; stand firm therefore, and do not submit again to a yoke of slavery."[5]

- **God created us to feast.** "On this mountain the LORD of hosts will make for all peoples a feast of rich food, a feast of well-aged wine, of rich food full of marrow, of aged wine well refined."[6]

- **God created us to show hospitality.** "Do not neglect to show hospitality to strangers, for thereby some have entertained angels unawares."[7]

- **God created us to spread positivity.** "The light of the eyes rejoices the heart, and good news refreshes the bones."[8]

- **God created us to dream big dreams.** "Now to him who is able to do far more abundantly than all that we ask or think, according to the power at work within us."[9]

## The Gospel Challenges Enthusiasts

The gospel also provides specific challenges to Enthusiasts. Now we'll explore the most common lies Sevens believe and see how the Bible provides much better

---

2   1 Thessalonians 5:16-18

3   Psalm 47:1

4   Psalm 107:9

5   Galatians 5:1

6   Isaiah 25:6

7   Hebrews 13:2

8   Proverbs 15:30

9   Ephesians 3:20

promises and blessings. We will move deeper into each of these throughout the next 40 days.

- **Lie #1: I need more to be happy.** The life of an Enthusiast is marked by a longing for *more*. Their deadly sin, or vice, is *gluttony*—an insatiable appetite for all things new: ideas, sexual encounters, relationships, travel, or possessions. While these are not bad in and of themselves, they'll never be enough. This pursuit leaves the Seven hungrier than before as they devour rather than digest God's gifts. But Jesus said He came so "that my joy may be in you, and that your joy may be full."[10] When you live from Christ's joy rather than for your joy, you cultivate the Seven's virtue of *sobriety* ("less is more"), which looks like living with balance, taking only what you need right now, choosing quality over quantity, and being fully present in the moment.

- **Lie #2: The future is more fulfilling.** The focus for Sevens is *planning* for the future, spending hours daydreaming or preparing for the next big thing in their lives. They fear that if they slow down and stop running, they'll sink into the present quicksand of boredom, sadness, discomfort, or other pains too difficult to bear. But keeping your head in the future will limit the fullness of life God wants you to experience today. The truth is our joy is not found in new plans, but in God's presence.[11] Joy is not an external pursuit but an internal fruit of the Holy Spirit that grows as we abide in Jesus.[12] Therefore, you can get excited just as much about today as you can tomorrow, for "this is the day that the LORD has made; let us rejoice and be glad in it."[13]

- **Lie #3: The grass is greener on the other side.** More than any other Enneagram type, Sevens have a fear of missing out (FOMO). This comes from one of their core fears which is *deprivation*, rooted in a feeling they will always be on their own, with no one to take care of them. But the healing message for Sevens comes from Jesus who said "do not be anxious about your life" because your heavenly Father takes care of your needs every day just like the birds of the

---

10    John 15:11

11    Psalm 16:11

12    Galatians 5:22-23

13    Psalm 118:24

air.[14] Since God will take care of you no matter where you are, the grass is not actually greener on the other side but wherever you choose to stick around and water it. Knowing this is the path to true contentment.

- **Lie #4: I need to stay positive.** Sevens are a gift to the world, radiating God's joy and enthusiasm for life. However, this role gets exaggerated when they start to believe they are more likable or lovable when they are fun and optimistic. Sevens are tempted to believe the world rewards those who are fine and upbeat, so they keep telling others "I'm okay." This leads them to sew fig leaves that say, "Don't worry, be happy!" to cover up any sadness, pain, or feelings of guilt and shame. But the truth is Jesus died on the cross for you—for your flawed self, not your fun, positive, crafted self. You are not worthy of love and care because you are the life of the party but because you belong to Him.

- **Lie #5: It's not okay to feel pain.** Sevens avoid pain and suffering like the plague. That's why they deploy pain-reducing strategies, such as deflecting uncomfortable questions through storytelling or humor, intellectualizing their feelings or putting them on the backburner, or reframing negatives into positives. But as C.S. Lewis reminds us, pain is not a looming threat, but God's megaphone to wake us up.[15] It serves as a teacher, guiding us to learn from our mistakes and discover areas of our hearts that require healing. When we take up our cross and follow our Suffering Savior courageously through the pain, rather than seeking shortcuts, we become better equipped to hold space for the grief of others and show more empathy and compassion.

- **Lie #6: I need to be free to be safe.** Another of the Seven's core fears is being *limited*. This causes Sevens to pursue autonomy and independence, which leads to an avoidance of commitments, responsibilities, routines, rules, structures, workplace hierarchies, or anything else that feels restrictive or confining. The Seven's defense mechanism of rationalization allows them to remove or stretch the boundary markers imposed on them by God or others and then justify (or spiritualize) their decisions as good. Though it feels counterintuitive, accepting our human and God-given limitations actually enhances pleasure rather than

---

14   Matthew 6:25-26

15   Clyde S. Kilby, *The Christian World of C. S. Lewis* (Grand Rapids, MI: William B. Eerdmans Publishing Company, 1995), 68.

diminishes it. Rather than wrestling for our freedom out of fear, we can have peace of mind knowing Jesus found joy by forgoing His freedom while He was here, not by holding onto it.

As you can see, the gospel will challenge your perception of the protagonists and antagonists in your life. In the Enthusiast's Neverland, positive-thinking is rewarded and Debbie Downers are punished. Your heroes are intriguing, interesting, adventurous, compromising, and avoid bringing up uncomfortable topics. They also never say no when you make a request or express a desire to do something. Likewise, your villains become those Pharisee-types who exhibit pessimism, demand too much, disregard the importance of fun, lack enthusiasm, discourage rule-bending, or hastily dismiss your ideas.

God's kingdom will not be filled with those who use Christ's freedom as an excuse for self-indulgence but by men and women who embrace the opportunity to serve others.[16] In this place, we exchange living in extremes for balance, impulsiveness for reliability, toxic positivity for empathy, and we take the path of suffering without shortcuts. In this place, we value simplicity over excess, see pain as a teacher rather than an adversary, acknowledge mourning alongside rejoicing, and confront fears rather than avoid them. In this place, we recognize true peace and joy is not found in future plans but in the presence of God—and we put anxiety to rest.

### The Invitation

When Jesus Christ, the divine all in all, entered into flawed and limited human history, He started His mission with an invitation: "The time is fulfilled, and the kingdom of God is at hand; repent and believe in the gospel."[17] He explained that to enter the good, eternally renewing life that begins well before the grave, you must do two things: believe the truth and turn from sin. Believing includes acknowledging who God is, who He says we are, and what He has done for us. More than that, to truly believe in a Christlike way is to *actively live into* those acknowledgments. Turning includes shedding our false worldview, misplaced desires, strong defenses, hide-and-seek strategies, and self-salvation efforts.

---

16  Galatians 5:13

17  Mark 1:15

If you are ready to begin this incredible 40-day journey and accept God's invitation, then let's go! It will be an enlightening ride of rapid growth as you become more self-aware and experience newfound freedom. You will encounter many light-bulb moments as you read profound truths for your type—and maybe even learn something about the people around you. The things you learn about yourself in this book will stick with you for the rest of your life.

## Three Types of Enthusiasts

To further explore how Sevens can look very different from one another, please check out the "Three Types of Enthusiasts" in the back of this book. These "subtypes" are helpful in understanding the nuances of the Enthusiast and will explain why some truths in this devotional will hit home more than others. If you are a Social Seven for example, you will look a lot like a Two and appear less selfish than other Sevens. These descriptions are meant to help you further uncover the unconscious motivations driving your behavior and may even help you discover why you're often confused with other Enneagram types!

# Free to Be You

*And David danced before the Lord with all his might.*

—2 Samuel 6:14

---

ONE OF MY FAVORITE, MOST EMBARRASSING STORIES takes place in the little trendy breakfast spot where my church's staff regularly met. All the other people at the restaurant were enjoying their meals when I suddenly stood up and yelled at the top of my lungs for everyone's attention. People paused their enjoyable conversations so I could inform them it was my fortieth birthday and it would mean the world to me if everyone would sing "Happy Birthday." After a brief moment of contemplation, to my surprise, everyone began singing!

As the final notes rang out, my co-pastor and best friend Alex sat in his chair laughing. You see, it wasn't actually my fortieth birthday--I just lost a bet. Alex had persuaded our team to play a card game during our weekly meeting—as Sevens usually get their way—with the stakes being that the loser had to do something embarrassing. For instance, one week, our worship leader had to jump into our

> The party don't start 'til I walk in.
>
> –Kesha[1]

---

1   "TiK ToK," AZ Lyrics, accessed on November 26, 2022, https://www.azlyrics.com/lyrics/keha/tiktok.html.

trash dumpster for a photo shoot and another, our worship intern had to sing "I'm a little teapot" in his most operatic voice. And well, you already know what happened to me. (Apparently, Alex not only could get everyone to do things, but he never lost!)

Enneagram Sevens, the Enthusiasts, are fun loving, high energy, life-givers who march to the beat of their own drums. You don't think outside of the box—you question that there ever was one. You bend the rules and do things differently than everyone else. And that's a *good* thing. But I know it's not always easy. Do you ever get the "look" from overly serious people? You know the one—the look that makes you feel guilty for being *you*?

Pastor Matthew Brown, in his book, *A Book Called YOU*, tells Sevens that King David also got the "look" from his wife.[2] After returning the ark to Jerusalem, David did a little celebration dance in the streets. Michal, angry with her husband, said, "How the king of Israel honored himself today, uncovering himself today before the eyes of his servants' female servants, as one of the vulgar fellows shamelessly uncovers himself!"[3]

> In God's presence, you are free to be you.

Have you ever done something with good intentions that someone immediately labeled as immodest, audacious, or disgraceful? David understood the feeling! However, he knew his celebration was the exact right action for the moment. Undeterred by his wife's embarrassment, David upped the ante, saying, "… I will celebrate before the LORD. I will become even more undignified than this … ."[4]

Like David, you don't have to apologize for being you. As Shauna Niequist shared with Enneagram teacher Suzanne Stabile,

> "The most helpful thing for me in learning the spiritual aspect of the Enneagram was giving myself permission to not do it the way the Fours in my life do it. My mom and my husband are Fours. They are

---

2   Matthew Stephen Brown, *A Book Called YOU: Understanding the Enneagram from a Grace-Filled, Biblical Perspective* (Nashville, TN: W Publishing, 2021), 130.

3   2 Samuel 6:20 (Speaking of dancing, did you ever hear why the Baptists don't like sex? Answer: Because it might lead to dancing! I love that joke. Okay, back to the story.)

4   2 Samuel 6:21-22 NIV

both introverts. They're deep thinkers and deep feelers, and they're contemplative by nature. I'm a party-thrower by nature. That looks a lot less spiritual to a lot of people. But I would say the first thing was giving myself permission to not be like a desert mystic and instead to offer my greatest gift, spiritual or not, which is hospitality. I think it's one of the ways God uses my life, and I have a disproportionate amount of joy when I practice hospitality. It makes me unreasonably happy. If I sell X amount of books, I'm like, 'That's good,' but a really meaningful dinner party is like, 'I believe in God and I believe He's good.' "[5]

***The Good News for Enthusiasts*** is that you don't have to fit into anyone's box because God accepts you—*all* of you—without any box required. In God's presence, you are free to be you, with all of your exuberant passion, funny quirks, unconventional methods, and your unique spiritual path. You can sing, dance, and get "undignified" in the eyes of the world because your boundless energy is not too much for Him.

---

### → Pray

Father, thank You for creating me the way You did. It's hard not to get insecure when others scold, label, or try to put me in a box. I will keep dancing and not be afraid to look "undignified" in the eyes of the world when I do these things as an act of worship in Your presence. Remind me that I am not outlandish in Your eyes; I am a beloved child.

---

5    Suzanne Stabile, *The Path Between Us: An Enneagram Journey to Healthy Relationships* (Downers Grove, IL: InterVarsity Press, 2018), 179-180.

# Day 1 Reflections:

**What do you love about the way God created you?**

**How free do you feel today to just be you? What or who might be holding you back?**

**When have you received that serious "look" from someone after just being you? How does it feel knowing God has a smile on His face and accepts every part of you?**

---

**➜ Respond**

Search for, listen to, and meditate on the song "Seven" from the Sleeping At Last project, Atlas: II.[6]

---

6   "Atlas: Year Two." Sleeping At Last. Accessed June 21, 2023. https://www.sleepingatlast.com/atlas.

# Jesus Keeps the Party Going

*These things I have spoken to you, that my joy may*

*be in you, and that your joy may be full.*

—John 15:11

---

WHEN IT WAS TIME FOR OUR ANNUAL church staff retreat, I suggested to my co-pastor Alex that we go to a nearby monastery. In *my* head, our team would spend deep, reflective alone time with the Lord along the tranquil lake shore on the grounds, and then come together to bond over what we heard. But as soon as *he* heard "retreat," what came to Alex's mind was spending time and having fun at the lake. And, because Alex is a persuasive Seven, our team ended up renting the lake house. (To his credit, I did get my deep encounter with the Lord there; it just wasn't in a pew, but in a kayak on the lake.)

> Joy is a net of love by which you can catch souls.
>
> —Mother Teresa[1]

People often think of Jesus as a man dressed in a robe hanging out in a monastery—like the one I wanted to go to. While Jesus does have a serious side, many overlook His joyful qualities. Why is

---

1    Martha Grace Reese, *Unbinding Your Soul: Your Experiment in Prayer & Community* (St. Louis, MO: Chalice Press, 2009), 83.

it so easy to forget that Jesus' first recorded miracle was turning water into wine? The *best* wine I might add! Weddings in those days were much like my college fraternity parties: people drank the best stuff first and the cheap kinds last (not always in moderation). But at the wedding party Jesus crashed, the confused host, after tasting the Messiah's vintage said, "Everyone serves the good wine first, and when people have drunk freely, then the poor wine. But you have kept the good wine until now."[2] I love the very next line: "This, the first of his signs, Jesus did at Cana in Galilee, and manifested his glory."[3] I guess Jesus is the King of the Jews and the brews. Glory!

While I was a campus minister with Cru, I wrote a Bible study for college students on the gifts of God and one of the lessons was on alcohol. I pointed out that Saint Gall, a missionary to the Celts, was better known for his brewing than preaching. After Charlemagne's reign, it was the *monks*, not atheists, who became Europe's protectors of sacred texts and sacred brews.[4] Many Christian traditions are entwined with alcohol, from the "bride's ale" (bridal) given to new brides to the mead (honey wine) provided to a couple to sustain them over their first moon cycle of marriage (their honeymoon). Theologian John Calvin's annual salary package included upwards of 250 gallons of wine, not books, and his contemporary, Martin Luther loved his ale almost as much as his freedom from the law.

> Joy is an internal fruit, not an external pursuit.

Anyway, the idea here is that, first, alcohol or any gift from God such as relationships, time, money, sex, is not the problem. As Martin Luther pointed out, "Do not suppose that abuses are eliminated by destroying the object which is abused? Men can go wrong with wine and women. Shall we then prohibit and abolish women?"[5] While it's true that alcohol has had a devastating effect on many lives, Luther's point is that our root problem lies in the heart.

---

2   John 2:10

3   John 2:11

4   It wasn't until the 19th century that modern science possessed the tools to see microscopic organisms like yeast, so the monks called the mysterious substance that fermented their grain water into beer simply *godisgoode*: "bicause it cometh of the grete grace of God." Kate Colquhoun, *Taste: The Story of Britain Through Its Cooking* (London, UK: Bloomsbury Publishing, 2012), 49.

5   Roland Herbert Bainton, *Here I Stand: A Life of Martin Luther* (Peabody, MA: Hendrickson Publishers, 2009), 213.

The takeaway for Enthusiasts is that only in Jesus will you find the joy you are truly longing for—without all the side effects. The harder you chase pleasurable experiences or materialistic things for their own sake, the more uncomfortable the happiness hangover will be the next day. So listen closely: *Joy is an internal fruit, not an external pursuit.* The joy you are really looking for is a fruit of the Holy Spirit that comes through abiding in Jesus.[6] So enjoy the gifts but find lasting delight in the Giver.

***The Good News for Enthusiasts*** is Jesus is not some cosmic killjoy but the opposite. When Jesus appeared He said, "These things I have spoken to you, that my joy may be in you, and that your joy may be full."[7] Jesus even endured the most painful of deaths "for the joy that was set before him"[8] to have *you* in heaven. He literally died to keep the party going! When you put your trust in Jesus, you never have to be afraid of missing out on the best of life because His joy is the kind that will bubble up from within, regardless of what time you show up to the party.

---

### → Pray

Father, thank You for being a life-giver and not a killjoy. The enemy tries to steal my joy, but it is secure in Your Son, Jesus. Remind me that joy is not attached to Your gifts but rests in You as the Giver. Keep my feet from wandering toward new things or experiences and plant them right here in the present because "in your presence there is fullness of joy."[9]

---

6   Galatians 5:22-23

7   John 15:11

8   Hebrews 12:2

9   Psalm 16:11

# Day 2 Reflections:

**Which gifts of God do you enjoy the most?**

---

**When have you chased one of God's gifts to the point of feeling empty, depressed, or regretful?**

---

**How is pursuing joy in external things different from living from Christ's joy?**

---

> **→ Respond**
>
> Plan some quality time with God (on a lake perhaps?) that remains true to you as a Seven. You don't have to go to a monastery. But make it fun and focused.

# Let There Be Fireworks

*In the beginning, God created the heavens and the earth. The earth*

*was without form and void, and darkness was over the face of*

*the deep. And the Spirit of God was hovering over the face of the*

*waters. And God said, "Let there be light," and there was light.*

—Genesis 1:1-3

---

THE LATIN WORD FOR JOY IS *GAUDIUM*, which also connotes *light*.[2] Enthusiasts are attracted to the light, being drawn to fun, excitement, and fireworks![3] You yourself are radiant, light-hearted, and entertaining, always lighting up the room wherever you go—figuratively and literally. I was dancing with my wife at a wedding reception a few months ago when I heard a girl next to me ask enthusiastically, "Should I go get my glow sticks out of the car? I keep them in there at all times, just in case." I

> Culture, then, is the furniture of heaven.
>
> —Andy Crouch[1]

---

1 Andy Crouch, *Culture Making: Recovering Our Creative Calling* (Downers Grove, IL: InterVarsity Press, 2009), 170.

2 Jerome Peter Wagner, *Nine Lenses on the World: The Enneagram Perspective* (Evanston, IL: NineLens Press, 2010), 375.

3 Ibid., 384.

try not to typecast people, but if there was a motto for Sevens, it would be "Glow sticks, just in case."

In the beginning, the Creator said to the darkness, "Let there be light."[4] Hovering above the waters of uncreated chaos, God imagined new possibilities and began painting, sculpting, and singing creation into existence. With His unfathomable knowledge and limitless power, rocks, animals, trees, mathematical formulas, scientific laws, and sexuality were written into existence. In the second creation story in Genesis, God sculpted man and woman from the dirt and filled them with His divine Spirit in one breath. The Eternal Artist stepped back and delighted in His workmanship.

You and I were created to enjoy and imitate God as His entrepreneurs. He gave mankind the task of stewarding creation—creating and cultivating new opportunities and endless possibilities.[5] Tailors, janitors, electricians, teachers, and composers all take the raw materials of fabric, brooms, electricity, the alphabet, and sound waves and emulate the Creator by turning them into something marvelous.[6]

> You were made in God's image to be a creator, not a consumer.

All that to say, you were made in God's image to be a *creator*, not a *consumer*. Unhealthy Sevens simply run after noise and shiny things, scrolling endlessly on their phones and absorbing entertainment. But healthy Sevens view themselves as culture makers, like Adam and Eve, who weren't merely amused by the animals in the garden but named them.[7]

I believe Sevens are the most natural culture makers on the Enneagram. Rather than being a thermometer reflecting the temperature of the room, you are a thermostat that turns up the heat with your dynamic presence everywhere you go. You build a family-like culture, embodying the Spirit filling you that draws people toward life-giving community. Chris, who recruited me to serve as a

---

4  Genesis 1:3

5  Genesis 1:28

6  Timothy Keller, *Every Good Endeavor: Connecting Your Work to God's Work* (New York City, NY: Penguin Books, an imprint of Penguin Random House, 2016), 47.

7  Genesis 2:20

pastor with him at my first church post, asked our whole team to do push-ups every week after our staff meeting, causing us to cheer and yell at each other with excitement. As a lead pastor, you won't find Chris hiding out before the Sunday gathering but outside, giving members high-fives as they walk into the building. He has used his charisma and catalytic gifts to multiply countless small groups out of his home and recruit new leaders who have started over a dozen autonomous churches over the last decade. Chris is a culture maker, not a consumer.

Resist the temptation to live for "fun and games," becoming someone who just purchases and uses up goods and services on this earth. Instead, leverage your amazing superpowers to design, speak, write, or start a new small group, community, non-profit, or cause––then find good people who can help you bring these great seeds to full bloom.

***The Good News for Enthusiasts*** is found in the words of Jesus: "I am the light of the world. Whoever follows me will not walk in darkness, but will have the light of life."[8] Our sin causes this world to turn cold, sad, boring, and lifeless. But Jesus, the Light of the world, overcame the darkness—not by being a consumer, but by being consumed on the cross. He chose to go through the valley of death to bring you new life. And right now, Jesus is *making all things new* and inviting you into the joy of doing it with Him. Today, hear His words: "You are the light of the world. A city set on a hill cannot be hidden."[9] God did not give you your trademark joy to hide behind a screen but to get out into the world and overcome the darkness that remains.

---

### → Pray

Father, thank You for giving me the capacity to feel joy to the extent that I do. Don't let me squander my joy by consuming pleasure in a selfish way, but help me to harness it and cause an explosion of good gifts for all people to enjoy. Remind me that I am filled with the life-giving breath of Your Holy Spirit, so I may be focused and disciplined in following through on the ideas you've given me.

---

8   John 8:12

9   Matthew 5:14

# Day 3 Reflections:

**What do you do to light up a room? When have others benefited from your dynamic presence?**

**How much of your energy is going toward consuming (taking things in) versus creating (putting things out)?**

**Where can you focus your enthusiasm and create something new to bless others?**

---

**→ Respond**

Keep a journal or file on your device of all your ideas. Write down new ideas as they come to you, but don't forget to circle back around and follow through on the ones that stick.

# You and King Solomon

*At Gibeon the Lord appeared to Solomon in a dream by*

*night, and God said, "Ask what I shall give you."*

—1 Kings 3:5

---

WHAT WOULD YOU DO IF GOD ALLOWED you to ask for whatever you wished? I can't think of any better question to ask an Enthusiast! Seriously, if someone asked you that question (and you couldn't wish for more wishes!), how would you answer? When King Solomon faced this question, he told God his greatest desire was a wise and discerning mind.[2] Delighted by his answer, God replied, "I give you also what you have not asked, both riches and honor, so that no other king shall compare with you, all your days."[3] Wow! Wisdom, wealth, *and* honor? Let's go!

> I hope everybody could get rich and famous and will have everything they ever dreamed of, so they will know that it's not the answer.
>
> –Jim Carrey[1]

---

1  "A Thought." The Knoxville News-Sentinel, June 22, 2007, Quote Page B4, Column 3, Knoxville, Tennessee. (Newspapers.com).

2  1 Kings 3:12

3  1 Kings 3:13

Like a Seven, King Solomon was a future-oriented visionary with a thirst for stimulating people and experiences. He was a judge, poet, governor, and entrepreneur who created many bold plans for his kingdom and truly believed he could actualize all of them. Solomon displayed the amazing networking skills of a Seven by doing the impossible—making an alliance with the pharaoh, king of Egypt, by marrying his daughter.[4] He was intelligent, wise, and witty: traits that impressed commoners and royalty alike, as we see in the famous visit from the Queen of Sheba.

However, while we may all be sitting back, impressed by your seemingly endless capacity for new experiences and acquiring new skills, you must become aware of the Seven's primary vice: *gluttony*, or the desire to always seek *more*. Solomon was living the average Seven's dream, with all the love, adoration, riches, success, and fame you could ask for. However, we start to notice some backsliding from the heights of wisdom and discernment when we learn Solomon spent seven years building the temple as a house for the Lord but took *thirteen* to construct his palatial home—nearly twice the amount of time!

> Solomon's lust for more corrupted an entire nation.

His backsliding eventually turned into a slippery slope: "As Solomon grew old, his wives turned his heart after other gods, and his heart was not fully devoted to the LORD his God."[5] Though Solomon's story began well, his people-pleasing and bottomless craving for more led him to build temples for his foreign wives. Perhaps, like an average Seven, he positively reframed this disobedient direction as a "peace-making strategy" for the flourishing of his religiously pluralistic kingdom. Regardless, we know Solomon's lust for more corrupted an entire nation, setting them on a collision course with exile.

At the end of Solomon's life, we hear the wise one say, "All is vanity."[6] Hang onto those words. We should thank Solomon for giving us this lesson and countless other teachings through his tradition of wisdom literature. The book of Proverbs, for example, beautifully displays the amazing contribution every Seven can make

---

4   1 Kings 3:1

5   1 Kings 11:4 NIV

6   Ecclesiastes 1:2

if they get focused, grounded, and committed. No matter what others think, you are not just the fun friend and leader but someone who possesses incredible intelligence and potential.

***The Good News for Enthusiasts*** is "something greater than Solomon is here."[7] A new King was born in Solomon's line, who resisted the gluttony of unending novelty and pleasure. Though King Solomon was born in a palace and had many servants, this new King was born in a stable and became a servant to all. Though King Solomon built himself a mansion, this new King promised to build you a mansion in heaven.[8] When you follow this new and better King, you will receive the pleasure of a life well-lived, rather than emptiness and vanity in your final days. As a Seven, let this third verse from the eighteenth-century hymn "Come Thou Fount of Every Blessing" be your daily prayer:

O to grace how great a debtor
Daily I'm constrained to be!
Let that grace now, like a fetter,
Bind my wandering heart to Thee.
Prone to wander, Lord, I feel it,
Prone to leave the God I love;
Here's my heart; O take and seal it;
Seal it for Thy courts above.

---

### → Pray

Father, thank You for giving me the life of Solomon in the Scriptures to learn how to live without regrets. Rein me in when I blindly pursue things that may turn my heart away from You. Give me the Spirit's power to remain focused to follow through on important projects so that others may benefit in the future.

---

7   Matthew 12:42

8   John 14:2

# Day 4 Reflections:

**If you could ask God for anything right now, what would it be?**

**In what ways does Solomon's story resonate with yours?**

**How have you seen God mature you in some of the areas where Solomon struggled?**

> **→ Respond**
>
> Memorize the third verse of "Come Thou Fount of Every Blessing."

# Day 5:

# Joie De Vivre

*So God created man in his own image, in the image of God*

*he created him; male and female he created them.*

—Genesis 1:27

---

THERE'S A POPULAR FRENCH PHRASE THAT LITERALLY translates as *the joy of living*: *joie de vivre* (pronounced zhwah-duh-veev) originates from the author Émile Zola's book of the same title. By the early 1900s, Zola's phrase spread from France to the rest of Europe and eventually into the English language. Someone full of *joie de vivre* embraces life enthusiastically and takes enormous delight in simply being alive. Every Enthusiast I know exudes *joie de vivre*.[9]

> We are each of us like a small mirror in which God searches for His reflection.
>
> –St. John Vianney

Do you realize others can see God more clearly through your personality? God created all of us as "mirrors" to reflect different aspects of His heart and character to a broken, hurting world. We are truly the *imago Dei*, translating the infinite, invisible

---

9   Grammarist, "Joie de vivre." Grammarist, accessed December 2022, https://grammarist.com/phrase/joie-de-vivre/.

One for a finite, visible world. When walking in the Spirit, you are optimistic, enthusiastic, spontaneous, charming, imaginative, versatile, entertaining, creative, appreciative, engaging, and playful.

Pause for a moment and read that list again.

You are a remarkable reflection of God's joy and abundance.[10]

Spiritual director and Enneagram author Marilyn Vancil teaches, "Sevens reflect the presence of God's joy and redemption in all of life. They envision a bright future where suffering is alleviated and all people are free to enjoy the limitless pleasures God provides. They view the world through a lens of abundance, and their enthusiasm is contagious. Type Sevens long to experience God's deep joy and expansiveness and join with others in the adventure of living life to the full."[11]

But as you know, it's impossible to reflect those characteristics of God at all times. The apostle Paul said the mirror was cracked from top to bottom when we exchanged the glory of God for the glory of man.[12] And it's not even a mistake relegated to people of the past; it's something we all do still. When walking in the flesh, those positive attributes turn sour, and you will find yourself being scattered, reckless, naive, impulsive, superficial, hedonistic, restless, escapist, unreliable, excessive, and childish.

> You are a remarkable reflection of God's joy and abundance.

Now pause for a moment and breathe! I'm not saying you are all of those things all of the time, but this list includes what Sevens self-report as their primary struggles when they aren't keeping in step with the Spirit, and we'll touch on each of these in future devotions.

When you drift from the gospel promise that you are worthy because of Christ, you will work hard to present a favorable image to the world that says, "I am lovable because I'm fun and optimistic." When unhealthy, you become a master

---

10  Marilyn Vancil, *Self to Lose Self to Find: Using the Enneagram to Uncover Your True, God-gifted Self* (New York: Convergent, 2020), 113.

11  Ibid., 113.

12  Romans 1:23

sculptor, picking up the chisel and carving the perfect "positive" persona that is high-spirited, interesting, multi-talented, and friendly, rather than serious, sad, or dull. You believe the lie that nobody will care about you unless the happy face remains front and center—no being down and out for you! You are tempted to believe the world rewards those who are fine and upbeat, so you keep telling yourself and others "I'm okay."[13] But you and I both know pretending to always be okay *isn't* okay.

I know it's tiring to play the role of entertainer all the time, secretly wishing someone else would step up to energize the room. I know deep down you wish you wouldn't have to always paint your life in such bright colors but would have the freedom to make use of the darker tones as well—to be honest about your pain, anxiety, and problems. If others only see you as independent, without any needs they can fulfill, how will they take care of you?

***The Good News for Enthusiasts*** is Jesus died on the cross for you—for your flawed self, not your fun, positive, crafted self. You are not worthy because you are joyful, adventurous, or charismatic. You are, right now without any effort, the *imago Dei*. The Holy Spirit is working like a master sculptor to clear away the excess marble and reveal what God sees, that true form beneath the image you work so hard to present to others. The Creator and Sustainer of all loves you still. When He looks in your mirror, He sees the image of His Son reflected back and says, "with you I am well pleased."[14]

---

### → Pray

Father, relax my tendency to present a positive and upbeat image. Help me to take off the fig leaves and be more honest with You and others about the pain and anxiety I'm covering up. When I display the courage to be vulnerable, please use it to draw others to take care of my needs and step up to fulfill the role of energizer when I don't have energy.

---

13   Wagner, *Nine Lenses on the World*, 384.

14   Mark 1:11

# Day 5 Reflections:

**Which of these words most reflect the image of God in you: optimistic, enthusiastic, spontaneous, charming, imaginative, versatile, entertaining, creative, appreciative, engaging, or playful?**

**When did you start to believe the lie "I'm more lovable when I'm fun and optimistic"? What people or life experiences have reinforced that belief?**

**What do you fear would happen if you told someone today that you weren't okay? What is the best thing that could happen?**

---

**→ Respond**

Catch yourself trying to amp up the excitement and then ask if you're doing that to cover something up.

---

# Fan Into Flame

*For this reason I remind you to fan into flame the gift of God,*

*which is in you through the laying on of my hands, for God gave*

*us a spirit not of fear but of power and love and self-control.*

—2 Timothy 1:6-7

---

AS A FORMER VINYL MUSIC DEEJAY, I'M more inclined to listen to techno than rock music. But that doesn't stop me from rewatching the movie *School of Rock*, a high-octane comedy about an overly enthusiastic guitarist named Dewey Finn (played by Jack Black). When Dewey gets thrown out of his bar band, he poses as a substitute music teacher at a prestigious private elementary school. There, he teaches his students—some of whom are classical music savants—about rock music and takes them on a thrilling adventure, culminating in the local Battle of the Bands.[1] The kids get to experience learning the way it should be through their teacher's indomitable enthusiasm and watch him win over their overly serious parents and convince their

> I have no special talents. I'm only passionately curious.
>
> –Albert Einstein

---

1   Frederick Brussat and Mary Ann Brussat, "School of Rock," School of Rock | Film Review, accessed June 9, 2023, https://www.spiritualityandpractice.com/films/reviews/view/6624/school-of-rock.

uptight principal (Joan Cusack) to sing by the end of the movie. Dewey Finn shows us that fun and serving others can be two sides of the same coin.

In his second letter to young Timothy, the apostle Paul challenged his student in the faith not to let his fire die. Paul exhorted Timothy to "fan into flame" his God-given strengths. He was concerned that his protégé could—as we all do occassionally—become complacent, allowing his presence and contributions to become cold and lethargic. An attentive reader of the apostle's missive might ask themselves, "What would it look like for me to 'fan into flame the gift of God'?"[2]

At the top of your list of strengths is your energy and optimism. As Enneagram teacher Ian Cron so eloquently puts it: "Sevens are caffeinated from birth. They burst into any room with an exuberance that turns heads. Their eyes twinkle and their lips hint at the smile they're about to give you. Sevens are the pied pipers and raconteurs, the self-help gurus and sales reps who know what you need before you do and make you feel honored to buy it from them. The story they tell themselves could easily be titled At the End of the Rainbow—There's a Pot of More Rainbows (and a Blue Unicorn)."[3]

> Sevens are jacks of all trades.

Sevens are "experience curators" who host the best parties and allow friends and strangers to enjoy the hospitality of God. Like Paul's other student Barnabas, whose name means "son of encouragement,"[4] Sevens are life-givers who are "full of the Holy Spirit and of faith."[5] Their encouragement empowers us to be more of who God created us to be.

You help us to see the silver lining when we are held captive by life's circumstances: "Two prisoners looked out from prison bars; one saw mud, the other saw stars."[6] When life hands us lemons, most of us may try to make some lemonade; *you* use it to make frozen strawberry lemonade margaritas. Like a humidifier, your

---

2   2 Timothy 1:6

3   Ian Morgan Cron, *The Story of You: An Enneagram Journey to Becoming Your True Self* (New York, NY: HarperCollins, 2021), 178-179.

4   Acts 4:36

5   Acts 11:24

6   Jerome P. Wagner, *The Enneagram Spectrum of Personality Styles 2E* (New York City, NY: G&D Media, 2021).

humor keeps your home and workplace from getting dry, stuffy, and overly serious. Your wit is a gift to lift our spirits when we are sad and a healing balm when we are hurting. My friend Elvin is the only pastor I know who can do a death-bed hospital visit and get someone laughing before they enter into the joy of heaven. But Elvin's humor has also caused some people to leave our church. See, Sevens are also "Pharisee filters," revealing by the brightness of their presence the inconsistencies of others.

Sevens are jacks of all trades—polymath, multitasking generalists who are freakishly fast learners and gifted at brainstorming and synthesizing new information. You also acquire new skills with ease, making the rest of us envious as you pick up a new instrument, language, or something else to dazzle us with. With these talents, the sky's the limit when it comes to the occupations and opportunities you can pursue. The challenge will be choosing one (or two) and sticking with them.

***The Good News for Enthusiasts*** is that Christ's love enflames your capacity to be energetic, optimistic, risk-taking, humorous, hospitable, and multi-talented. Your natural gifts are part of a grand plan to restore humanity, mirroring Christ's example of expending every ounce of His vitality, even to the point of death, to give us life. As Jesus said, "I came that they may have life and have it abundantly."[7] Your call is to show how to live out that abundance through all of life's joys and sorrows.

---

### → Pray

Father, like Timothy's mother and grandmother, I wouldn't be here without my friends and family. Thank You for giving me faithful people who have strengthened my faith and encouraged me to use my gifts. Help me to walk slowly through this world and be a life-giving presence, pouring out the fire of Your love on a world that's often negative and joyless.

---

7  John 10:10

# Day 6 Reflections:

**Paul asked Timothy to take inventory of the spiritual deposit made by his mother and grandmother. What spiritual truths and gifts have been passed down to you from your family and/or mentors?**

**Which of those strengths have been affirmed the most throughout your life?**

**What's one thing you can do to ignite and develop your gifts?**

> **→ Respond**
>
> Identify your strengths and give examples of how you are already using them.

# The Seven-Movie Genre

*You make known to me the path of life; in your presence there is*

*fullness of joy; at your right hand are pleasures forevermore.*

—Psalm 16:11

WHAT IS YOUR FAVORITE MOVIE GENRE? ACCORDING to author Judith Searle, Enthusiasts tend to love adventure and sci-fi movies. She provides a few unwritten rules for stories typifying Sevens: The Seven protagonist is driven by an appetite for new adventure, is generally charming and reckless (although somehow they always escape serious injury and death), and is a highly intelligent bon vivant who enjoys good food, good drink, and has numerous lovers. However, their self-indulgence limits their capacity to commit to a person or principle and they often move from one adventure to the next with little change in their character.[1] Peter Pan is the quintessential Enthusiast,

> Everyone has oceans to fly, if they have the heart to do it. Is it reckless? Maybe. But what do dreams know of boundaries?
>
> –Amelia Earhart

---

1    Pace Smith, "Enneagram Story Genres, with Judith Searle." Wild Crazy Meaningful Enneagram, accessed June 9, 2023, https://pacesmith.com/wcme-028/.

whose fairytale life in Neverland, including fantastical pirates and a community literally called "the lost boys," puts a Seven's resistance to growing up and avoidance of responsibility on full display.

The biblical character Jonah tried to avoid responsibility by high-tailing it to Tarshish after the Lord told him to set up a revival tent in the enemy city of Nineveh. But going on the run ended up being more painful—with the man-swallowing fish and all. After the fish threw Jonah up on the beach, Jonah preached the sermon of his life in Nineveh, leading to a nation-wide revival. But the angry prophet didn't celebrate; rather, he threw a tantrum because he didn't get his way (something that an unhealthy Seven does quite often).

Does your sense of adventure cause you to lack commitment? Sevens want to keep their future options open, and when they finally *do* commit to something, often start thinking about what's next. Having to make a big commitment is so stressful for Sevens because it feels like you're giving away all the other options!

> You can't receive God's joy when you're seeking a substitute in the latest adventure.

Tara, a filmmaker, recognizes this pattern in her life: "It's unfortunately true that my tendency is to get very excited about something new, then get bored with it and not follow through. For me, variety is the spice of life. Talking about doing something 'interesting' makes me feel better, even if we don't do it. I like to learn new things. I love to take classes—whether it's cooking, or ballroom dancing, or rollerblading, whatever… . It's also been hard for me to commit to a relationship because I'm always looking for something that might be better, making sure I've checked out all my options."[2]

A lack of commitment and follow-through will cause real problems in your life and get you more stuck than you were before. Sevens generally have a long list of friendships or relationships with people who feel "ditched" by them because those people understood the relationship to be deeper than the Seven did.[3] Every time

---

2   Don Richard Riso and Russ Hudson, *The Wisdom of the Enneagram: The Complete Guide to Psychological and Spiritual Growth for the Nine Personality Types* (New York, NY: Bantam Books, 1999), 272-273.

3   Ibid., 169.

you quit or move on quickly to the next thing, you may send the (unintentional) message of, "I don't care about you." Therefore, the life-long growth path will be to stay committed to the relationships and assignments God calls you to beyond the honeymoon phase. To see progress, start with the small things first: being on time, finishing the small tasks you start, and honoring a plan or job description even when something shiny or new presents itself.[4]

***The Good News for Enthusiasts*** is that your joy is not found in new *pursuits*, but in God's *presence*. As David said, "You make known to me the path of life; in your presence there is fullness of joy; at your right hand are pleasures forevermore."[5] Memorize that verse! You can't receive God's joy when you're seeking a substitute in the latest adventure.

Though Jonah ran from his pain and "away from the presence of the LORD,"[6] Jesus stayed fully committed to His calling and relationships. He limited His options, often saying no to new opportunities so He could get to Jerusalem to finish what He started. Jesus purposefully "set toward Jerusalem," knowing the trials awaiting Him there at the hands of the spiritual and worldly authorities.[7] Though Jesus' life did not look like the fairytale, Peter Pan, abundant life to many, He drew joy from being in the Father's presence. Through many signs and miracles, He led His disciples on the wildest adventure, showing the only path to true abundance.

---

### → Pray

Father, thank You for giving me a great sense of adventure. I love being able to feel a heightened sense of pleasure with the life You've given me. Help me to remain as committed to You and others as You are with me. Replace my impulsivity with reliability as I find joy in Your presence, rather than imagining it as somewhere else in the distant future.

---

4   Stabile, *The Path Between Us*, 174-175.

5   Psalm 16:11

6   Jonah 1:3

7   Luke 9:53

# Day 7 Reflections:

**Which adventure will you pursue next? How will this impact the people who are relying on you now?**

**What is one commitment you've been running from or have backed out of recently?**

**How might your actions change knowing joy is not waiting in the next pursuit but in God's presence?**

> ## → Respond
>
> Create a timeline for committing to a relationship, group, project, location, or role you know will stretch you, and then ask someone to hold you accountable.

# Give Me Liberty or Death!

*Now the Lord is the Spirit, and where the Spirit of the Lord is, there is freedom.*

—2 Corinthians 3:17

PATRICK HENRY, ONE OF THE FOUNDING FATHERS of the United States, was a gifted communicator and major figure in the American Revolution. Motivating the American colonies to fight for independence from the British, he famously declared, "Give me liberty, or give me death!"[2] Such a rally cry sounds right flying from an Enthusiast's lips, as you would likely rather die than give up your independence.

> May we think of freedom, not as the right to do as we please, but as the opportunity to do what is right.
>
> –Peter Marshall Jr.[1]

In the biblical account of humanity's first couple, Adam and Eve were enjoying paradise, walking with God and experiencing the fullness of divinely intended joy, beauty, fruitfulness, and abundance. But when their enemy, the serpent,

---

1 Dan Miller and Jared Angaza, *Wisdom Meets Passion: When Generations Collide and Collaborate* (Nashville, TN: Thomas Nelson, 2012), 49.

2 History.com, "Patrick Henry," August 9, 2022, https://www.history.com/topics/american-revolution/patrick-henry.

slithered into their lives, he sought to kill and destroy the love and trust between Creator and Creation. In an instant, the great doubt was introduced—that heartbreaking question: *Is this really all there is? Is God holding out on me?*

As a result, Adam and Eve rebelled against a God who appeared to want to tie them down. Why would He not allow them to eat from the best-looking tree? Didn't He want them to experience the whole garden? They grasped for the fruit of freedom, this new shiny thing that promised to make life more exciting. Not wanting to miss out on what God had forbidden, they flipped the order of creation, which is to freely receive God's abundance with thanksgiving and instead *take* and eat the fruit.

Sevens love freedom and fear being limited or trapped. Their temptation is to be omnipresent like God, free to do all things and be in all places at one time. Sevens read, "Our God is in the heavens; he does all the he pleases,"[3] and think, *Why can't I have that life?* Sevens struggle more than any other number to accept their human and God-given limitations. They feel limited by time, wishing there were more days in the week to pursue all their plans. That's why they may give an enthusiastic *yes* to an invitation but bail out later when something better comes up. Sevens also feel limited by the fact there are things in life they just can't have! Depression rears its ugly head when a Seven ruminates on what they can't have or do.

When feeling trapped, average Sevens will attempt to "work cleverly around people or systems that they perceive will impose limitations on them or ask them to conform."[4] They will also go to great lengths not to get angry if they find themselves in a confining situation. Instead, they search for secret passageways or the nearest exit sign. But eventually, when feeling backed into a corner with no way out, they may take a superior stance and blame others for their troubles. Helen Palmer shares that being limited or trapped feels demeaning to a Seven and that their accusations are a sign of their struggle.[5]

---

3   Psalm 115:3

4   Cron, *The Story of You*, 187.

5   Helen Palmer, *The Enneagram in Love and Work: Understanding Your Intimate and Business Relationships* (New York,

***The Good News for Enthusiasts*** is "for freedom Christ has set us free."[6] Jesus was trapped in the grave so that you would be forever set free from it, gaining your liberty through His death. We have been set free from our sins and from the yoke of religion and man-made traditions that tie us down with unnecessary rules that take the joy out of life. We have also been set free from submitting to others' convictions that we may not need to share.

God delights in you being a jazz artist who doesn't want to stick to playing the same notes as everyone else but improvises and lives spontaneously. After all, "you were called to freedom."[7] But Paul also adds, "Only do not use your freedom as an opportunity for the flesh, but through love serve one another."[8] Your God-given freedom is not the kind that selfishly wants to have it all and do it all but limits itself to serving God and others in the same way your loving Savior did for you.

---

### → Pray

Father, I don't like being told what to do because I can't stand the feeling of being limited or trapped. Help me release the control I desire to have over my freedom and trust You fully with my life and decisions. Because Christ freely chose to live and die for me, I will walk in Your freedom rather than living for mine.

---

NY: HarperOne, 2010), 190.

6   Galatians 5:1

7   Galatians 5:13

8   Galatians 5:13

# Day 8 Reflections

**When have modern-day Pharisees tried to take away your freedom unjustly?**

**What kinds of things do you feel limited by? How do you usually respond to these real (or perceived) limitations?**

**How have your flights of freedom negatively impacted your loved ones or caused you to stray from God's path?**

---

### ➜ Respond

Because of your impulse to say "yes," practice telling someone "maybe" instead (or even an "I'll get back to you"!). Take some time to ask yourself how a "yes" might impact your family, add too much to your plate, or take you away from your current responsibilities.

# Stay in Your Lane

*And the Lord God commanded the man, saying, "You may surely eat of*

*every tree of the garden, but of the tree of the knowledge of good and evil*

*you shall not eat, for in the day that you eat of it you shall surely die."*

—Genesis 2:16-17

IF GOD CREATED US FOR FREEDOM, THEN why can't we do whatever we want? Why is the Bible filled with things we *can't* do? Well, for the same reason there are stripes on a running track—they keep everyone running in their lane without tripping everyone else up in the process. For example, the apostle Paul addressed those in the Corinthian church who carried a "I have the right to do anything" mindset. Their Christian liberty became an excuse to eat meat offered to idols in front of their brothers and sisters, fellow believers whose consciences wouldn't allow them to do the same. Paul reminded them that while it was lawful for them to eat this food biblically, it wasn't helpful if it tripped others up.[2]

> Anxiety is the dizziness of freedom.
>
> –Søren Kierkegaard[1]

---

1 Søren Kierkegaard, *The Concept of Anxiety: A Simple Psychologically Orienting Deliberation on the Dogmatic Issue of Hereditary Sin* (New York, NW: Liveright Publishing, 2014), 75.

2 1 Corinthians 10:23

If we didn't have street lanes or stoplights, there would be a lot more deaths on the road. I think that is at the heart of God's command not to eat from the tree of the knowledge of good and evil "for in the day that you eat of it you shall surely die."[3] As mentioned in yesterday's devotion, Enthusiasts desire the same freedom as God but (as with all fallible beings) cannot handle it in the same way without consequences. We are like fish who want the freedom of living on land but weren't designed to do so. Therefore, God's boundaries keep us from harm.

But boundaries were not established by God only for our *preservation* but for our *pleasure*. It's true that establishing boundaries within your sex life can help protect against STDs and prevent unwanted pregnancies, but they do so much more than that. Boundaries enhance pleasure rather than diminish it. As Pastor Ben Patterson explains, "The pleasures and goodness of sex are heightened, not lessened by proper restraint, in the same way the Colorado River is made more powerful by the walls of the Grand Canyon. The very narrowness of the river's channel there makes for a greater river. Farther south, as the river flows through the deserts of California and Arizona, it is shallow, wide, and muddy, even stinky in spots. Wider boundaries diminish the river; sharper, stronger, and narrower boundaries strengthen it. Less is more."[4]

> Boundaries were not established by God only for our preservation but for our pleasure.

Living within God's boundaries is like sitting next to a warm, cozy fire on a cold winter day. But when a Seven starts getting curious about all the fun things you can do with fire, they may downplay its power, ignore the natural boundaries of the fireplace, and take a log out to see what will happen. But eventually, playing with fire may cause the whole house to burn down.

Curiosity is a gift from God, but boundless curiosity (the kind that killed the cat) may take you into enemy territory. The serpent is the first one in the Bible to rationalize sin, tempting Adam and Eve to rebel against God's loving limits by widening the protective boundary markers around His clear commands.

---

3   Genesis 2:17

4   "The Goodness of Sex and the Glory of God," Desiring God, September 25, 2004, https://www.desiringgod.org/messages/the-goodness-of-sex-and-the-glory-of-god.

If you catch yourself doing this, it just might be because the enemy knows rationalization is the chink in the Seven's armor.

I know God's rules feel insufferably limiting at times and may be a painful experience to read them in your Bible or be reminded of them by your loved ones, but in the end they will save your life and relationships. Remember, joy is not found on the other side of the fence where the grass is greener but right in the middle of God's will.

***The Good News for Enthusiasts*** is though we've rationalized away God's boundary markers, bringing pain to ourselves or others, there is no condemnation for our prodigal past for those in Christ Jesus.[5] Jesus also forgives us for the times we move out of our lane to flaunt our freedom, bringing beer to the church event when everyone else is drinking soda or sweet tea, or laughing at others who watch Pureflix instead of Netflix. Remember, we have freedom of conscience and more often than not, we should follow its lead; but sometimes, freedom is best expressed in limiting ourselves for the sake of the community. Jesus won us over, not by flaunting His freedom, but by forgoing it.

---

### → Pray

Father, thank You for always having my best in mind. Though it feels suffocating at times to live within limits, remind me that Your boundaries always enhance rather than diminish my joy. Empower me by the Holy Spirit to forego my freedom when it will hurt and not help build someone's faith.

---

5  Romans 8:1

# Day 9 Reflections

**How do you rationalize to extend the boundary markers of God's clear commands? What do you often say to bend the rules or avoid responsibility?**

**When have you flaunted your freedom before in a dramatic way? How did it trip others up?**

**How did Jesus restrict His freedom in order to build us up?**

### → Respond

Ask someone you trust to point out when you rationalize—or find good excuses—to avoid accountability. Then prepare yourself to work through the pain that will arise when they do, rather than providing more justification.

# Living in the Matrix

*But the serpent said to the woman, "You will not surely die. For*

*God knows that when you eat of it your eyes will be opened,*

*and you will be like God, knowing good and evil."*

—Genesis 3:4-5

---

IN MY FAVORITE MOVIE OF ALL TIME, *The Matrix*, the rebel leader Morpheus offers Neo (played by Keanu Reeves) a choice between a red pill and blue pill. Morpheus says, "You take the blue pill—the story ends, you wake up in your bed and believe whatever you want to believe. You take the red pill—you stay in Wonderland, and I show you how deep the rabbit-hole goes."[2] Taking the blue pill represents living in ignorance in the machine-generated dream world's false reality. Taking the red pill represents living in a harsh reality full of difficulties, paradoxes,

> If you ignore a problem for long enough, it either goes away or ruins your life. So 50/50. Pretty good odds.
>
> —Enneagram 7[1]

---

1  (@thatenneagram7life). "Feelings? Yuck! I always thought I was comfortable." *Instagram*, September 4, 2021. https://www.instagram.com/p/CTaAk1nH0n0/.

2  "The Matrix (1999)," IMDb, accessed June 12, 2023, https://www.imdb.com/title/tt0133093/characters/nm0000401.

and insoluble problems. As you might have guessed, Neo chose the red pill and joined Morpheus in saving the world.

Every Enthusiast must choose between taking the blue pill (false reality) or red pill (reality). The Seven's defense mechanism, *rationalization*, will keep you living in a made-up world rather than the real one. As Beatrice Chestnut explains, rationalization "entails finding good reasons for doing whatever you want to do, seeing things however you want to see things, or believing whatever you want to believe."[3] It's the strategy the serpent used with Adam and Eve. He painted them a picture of a false reality, one where God was holding back from them and holding them back. By that logic, eating the fruit was justified because it wouldn't actually lead to death but enlightenment.

Sevens can use rationalization to justify sin and live guilt-free ("I stole a pen from work, but I didn't steal something of real value."), to not take responsibility ("I didn't finish, but it was a good learning experience."), or as a way to charm their way out of trouble ("I didn't do what you asked because I was offering moral support to my friend who's having a rough day. I know you'd do the same.").

> The Seven's defense mechanism, rationalization, will keep you living in a made-up world rather than the real one.

Like a magician or master of the Matrix who can bend a spoon using only their mind, so can a Seven bend our minds with their charm. No one does this better than Captain Jack Sparrow, who in the movie *Pirates of the Caribbean* says, "Me? I'm dishonest, and a dishonest man you can always trust to be dishonest. Honestly. It's the honest ones you want to watch out for, because you can never predict when they're going to do something incredibly … stupid."[4] What Captain Sparrow did is called *reframing*: a skill mastered by any self-respecting Seven.

---

3   Chestnut, *The Complete Enneagram*.

4   "Pirates of the Caribbean: The Curse of the Black Pearl (2003)," IMDb, accessed June 12, 2023, https://www.imdb.com/title/tt0325980/characters/nm0000136.

*Reframing* is putting a negative picture into a positive "frame" and this Seven superpower can be used for good. For example, when someone dies and a family member can't get over the loss, a Seven can reframe the situation by reminding them of our hope in the bliss of heaven and eventual reunification. A Seven's positive outlook on life is so good for our spiritual well-being!

But the dark side of reframing includes ignoring painful feelings or responsibilities Sevens don't want in their "matrix." Oftentimes, reframing is just a way of sheltering themselves from feeling guilt or embarrassment. For example, when they become unemployed, they tell others, "I've become a freelancer!" Another, more "spiritual" reframing is to relabel selfish pursuits (such as that short term mission trip to a vacation spot!) as "kingdom opportunities."

**The Good News for Enthusiasts** is God sees through the loopholes you use to justify getting what you want and avoiding what you don't. And He loves you still! He won't always respond the way you want, but He knows what you need. He will help you face your problems rather than brushing them off so that you can make better life decisions and learn to cope with challenging feelings—all of which will ultimately lead to greater growth. Just as Neo was supported by Morpheus, God will help you to survive in the real world, offer the tools to fight, and be by your side in the toughest battles. Best of all, He has given you the Spirit of Truth to help you to discern between "the matrix" and reality so that you can travel beyond the temporary bliss of ignorance to the ecstasy of God's eternal joy.

---

### → Pray

Father, convince me that reality is my friend. It's challenging to stop running, turn around, and look at the truth in the face. Oftentimes, I don't even know what I'm running from. Thank You for loving the real me behind the mask of charm that I present to the world. Help me to live in the real world like Jesus and depend on the Spirit to face all that comes my way.

# Day 10 Reflections

**When has reframing a negative into a positive helped someone who was cynical, depressed, or grieving?**

**How do you use charm, story-telling, or intellectual persuasion to deflect discomfort or maintain a positive outlook?**

**What are you reframing right now as a way to "not look so bad" or downplay negative results you're experiencing in the home or workplace?**

---

### ➔ Respond

Do a S.W.O.T. (Strengths, Weaknesses, Opportunities, Threats) analysis for a current project or future plan, but spend more time on the weaknesses and threats sections. Learn from the uncomfortable feelings that arise rather than brushing them off.

# It's All Good

*Jesus wept.*

—John 11:35

---

HAKUNA MATATA IS AN EAST AFRICAN TERM that literally means "no worries." The term was made popular in Disney's 1994 animated classic, *The Lion King*. Elton John and lyricist Tim Rice found it in a Swahili phrase book and wrote a song for the characters Timon the meerkat and Pumbaa the warthog. In Seven-like fashion, these two tried to cheer up young Simba who felt guilty for his father's death. They sang, "Hakuna Matata … it means no worries / For the rest of your days / It's our problem-free philosophy / Hakuna Matata!"[2]

> Keep your face to the sunshine and you cannot see the shadow.
>
> –Helen Keller[1]

Like Simba's new friends, Enthusiasts have an "It's all good," problem-free philosophy on life. As in the case of Timon and Pumbaa, healthy optimism is a great gift to us all—particularly through life's toughest moments. I'm sure someone with a Seven's view of joy amid pain recommended the

---

1   Elizabeth Wagele, *The Enneagram for Teens: Discover Your Personality Type and Celebrate Your True Self* (United States: PLI MEDIA, 2014).

2   "Hakuna Matata," Disney Fandom, accessed June 12, 2023, https://disney.fandom.com/wiki/Hakuna_Matata.

orchestra play music on the sinking Titanic's deck. Such strategies are indeed helpful during a crisis, so long as the Seven faces the reality that the ship *is* going down (rather than daydreaming about their part in the future bestselling movie).

In addition to the defense mechanism of *rationalization*, Sevens also use *idealization* and *sublimation*, which seem to run naturally in the background like an operating system's built-in programs. Idealization allows Sevens to perceive people and experiences as much better than they are to avoid dealing with flaws or uncomfortable emotions attached to them.[3] Meanwhile, sublimation is running to resist bringing difficult things into your conscious awareness. Like holding a beach ball underwater, you push things like conflict, aging, mortality, or the pain of separation out of sight and out of mind.[4]

Sevens are like moths that avoid the darkness and flock to the light. Once again— and I can't overstate this—your optimism is a true gift. It's what enabled Helen Keller, who was deaf, blind, and mute, to courageously overcome indescribable challenges and maintain a positive attitude. Keller famously said, "Keep your face to the sunshine and you cannot see the shadow."[5]

> Sevens are like moths that avoid the darkness and flock to the light.

Sevens are like helium balloons, pulling the rest of the world up toward the heavens with their optimism. But we can learn a valuable lesson studying helium: when inhaled (who doesn't want to talk like a chipmunk?) it displaces oxygen. Therefore, the more pure helium you inhale, the longer your body goes without critical oxygen, which quickly leads to death by asphyxiation.[6] (That gives a whole new meaning to the phrase "toxic" positivity!)

Toxic positivity may lead you to shame or guilt someone you think just needs to stay cheerful or maintain a sunny outlook on life at all times, even when the situation might call you to open yourself to pain or doubt. They are wonderful at

---

3  Chestnut, *The Complete Enneagram.*

4  Scott Loughrige, Clare M. Loughrige, Douglas A. Calhoun, and Adele Ahlberg Calhoun, *Spiritual Rhythms For The Enneagram: A Handbook for Harmony and Transformation* (Downers Grove, IL: InterVarsity Press, 2019), 179-180.

5  Wagele, *The Enneagram for Teens.*

6  "What Happens When You Inhale Helium?" Healthline, November 14, 2022, https://www.healthline.com/health/inhaling-helium#what-happens.

fulfilling half of Paul's exhortation to "rejoice with those who rejoice" but struggle mightily with the second piece: "weep with those who weep."[7] As opposed to positive thinking (which is truly good), such toxic positivity rejects all difficult emotions (in yourself or others) and replaces them with a cheerful facade.

As an action step, instead of saying things like "Just stay positive," or "It could be worse," or "Things happen for a reason," offering a simple, "I'm listening," or "Wow, that must really be hard," can bring all the comfort the moment needs. When you freely give your presence and validate others' feelings, you'll experience more authentic human connections with the people you love.

***The Good News for Enthusiasts*** is that Jesus was a kaleidoscope of emotions, rejoicing *and* mourning with others. When Jesus showed up at Lazarus' funeral, He comforted the family with tears, not toxic positivity.[8] Jesus, who became fully human, didn't carry an "It's all good" posture but plumbed the depths of the human experience so He could be fully present with us. Because your darker emotions aren't too much for Him, you can take off your cheerful mask and bring your full self to Jesus without fear of getting rejected. As the Psalmist said, "When the cares of my heart are many, your consolations cheer my soul."[9]

---

### → Pray

Father, I feel blessed to have the gift of optimism. I get great joy out of being drawn to the light and pointing others toward the same. Help me not to go too far and make others feel like they are doing something wrong if they aren't always happy. Use me to be fully present to listen to, cry with, and comfort others just like Jesus does with me.

---

7   Romans 12:15

8   John 11:35

9   Psalm 94:19

# Day 11 Reflections

**How has your optimism gotten you (or someone close to you) through some really tough times?**

**When have you avoided darker realities through idealization (perceiving someone or something as better than they are) or sublimation (pushing difficult things out of sight and mind)?**

**What will you do to avoid toxic positivity the next time someone goes through a difficult time?**

## → Respond

The first step to combating toxic positivity is to stop judging yourself when you feel sad or doubtful. Remember these emotions make you perfectly human.

# Stress Activators

*And Moses lifted up his hand and struck the rock with his staff twice, and*

*water came out abundantly, and the congregation drank, and their livestock.*

*And the Lord said to Moses and Aaron, "Because you did not believe in*

*me, to uphold me as holy in the eyes of the people of Israel, therefore you*

*shall not bring this assembly into the land that I have given them."*

—Numbers 20:11-12

WHAT MAKES YOU FEEL STRESSED OUT? SOME of the most common triggers Enthusiasts mention are feeling limited, restrained, dismissed, or not taken seriously. Other stressors include being around people who are too negative or pessimistic, don't value fun, don't share your enthusiasm, don't let you bend the rules, expect you to fix their problems, criticize you unjustly, or shoot down your ideas too quickly.

> No pressure, no diamonds.
> —Thomas Carlyle[1]

When these things happen, you may find yourself "suddenly" at the breaking point, ready to blow up in

---

1   Iam A. Freeman, *Seeds of Revolution: A Collection of Axioms, Passages and Proverbs, Volume 1* (Bloomington, IN: iUniverse, World Harvest, 2014), 74.

spectacularly public ways.[2] More than once, the humble-but-stressed-out Moses seemed to throw up his hands, telling God he would rather die than deal with the unfaithful Israelites another moment. While the tantrums often occurred in private, Moses' meltdowns took place before the entire nation—like the one at Meribah, when he struck the rock.[3]

Under stress, Sevens slide to the lower side of the Type One, becoming overly strict, rigid, demanding, and serious. You lose your light, whimsical nature, and place unrealistically high expectations on yourself or others. When this doesn't work, you may rebel and become scattered, flaky, and fidgety. As your anxiety grows (particularly if it remains unconscious), you become more impatient and begin comparing yourself to others, fixated on how deprived you are.

To combat this feeling of deprivation, average Sevens start to pester others until they get what they want. As Suzanne Stabile shares, "When Sevens really want something that is within your purview to give them, they are very persistent. It's like being pecked to death by chickens."[4]

> The next time you feel the kettle getting hot, slow down and bring your anxieties to Christ.

When pestering doesn't work, unhealthy Sevens will throw a tantrum. By acting in such a demanding way, they believe they may finally get what they want—and often do. My Seven friend admitted to me, "I throw pity parties in my head, blame everyone else, and make excuses for how it's really your fault, and you just don't really understand. Because if you really understood, you would see it my way."

***The Good News for Enthusiasts*** is that there is a way to bend without breaking. There will be times when you come to a breaking point because you spiral into an addiction, go through an experience you can't reframe positively, become severely fatigued or ill due to your fast pace or pursuing too many new endeavors, or encounter relational confrontations or interventions from family members or

---

2   Beth McCord and Jeff McCord, *Becoming Us: Using the Enneagram to Create a Thriving Gospel-Centered Marriage* (Nashville, TN: Morgan James Publishing, 2020).

3   Numbers 20:10-13

4   Stabile, *The Path Between Us*, 182.

friends.[5] But when these things happen, the God who is "merciful and gracious, slow to anger and abounding in steadfast love and faithfulness"[6] will restore you and make you stronger than before if you honestly bring your pain to Him and His community.

God is long-suffering, meaning He is willing to wait with patience long before showing anger. Because He has a long fuse, He does not throw a tantrum or run away from us but is merciful and forbearing. And just as Jesus was restrained unjustly on the cross yet reverberated love in a remarkable demonstration of self-control, you too can pour out grace on even the most negative and controlling people in your life. God is willing to give you a longer fuse so you can act honorably before all and "uphold [God] as holy in the eyes of the people"[7]—the very thing Moses failed to do at Meribah.

The next time you feel the kettle getting hot, slow down and bring your anxieties to Christ. Resolve to *stop and stay*, working through conflict with others, rather than fleeing. Ask clarifying questions rather than assuming they are purposefully trying to limit or deprive you. Remember, they may not share your enthusiasm for fun, freedom, or the future, but God loves them for who *they* are and for the unique gifts they bring. Show up for others, and trust Christ to show up for you.

### → Pray

Father, thank You for sending Your Son to be our example of someone who bent without breaking. Through temptation, opposition, persecution, and even death, He did not fold. Oh Lord, let the same compassion flow out of me that flowed out of Jesus when He was struck on the cross.

---

5   Cron, *The Story of You*, 188-189.

6   Psalm 86:15

7   Numbers 20:12

# Day 12 Reflections:

**What activates your stress most often? What is your usual response?**

**How can you address your anxiety now to prevent a public meltdown like the one Moses experienced?**

**Where in your past might you have experienced trauma that still needs to be addressed?**

---

### ➜ Respond

Because others may be able to see the warning signs before you do, ask someone to share how they can tell when you are stressed out.

# The Megaphone of Pain

*He was despised and rejected by men, a man of sorrows and*

*acquainted with grief; and as one from whom men hide their*

*faces he was despised, and we esteemed him not.*

—Isaiah 53:3

---

Tylenol is a life-saver isn't it? We take this over-the-counter medicine regularly to numb many of the nagging pains that come our way. In 2015, a team from Ohio State University did a study where 167 subjects were given either a dose of acetaminophen or a placebo and then were exposed to both negative and positive images. When compared to the placebo group, the subjects who took the real Tylenol not only described the unpleasant images as less emotionally arousing but the pleasant images too. The study

> God whispers to us in our pleasures, speaks in our conscience, but shouts in our pains: it is His megaphone to rouse a deaf world.
>
> —C.S. Lewis[1]

---

1    Clyde S. Kilby, *The Christian World of C. S. Lewis* (Grand Rapids, MI: William B. Eerdmans Publishing Company, 1995), 68.

concluded that, while its pain-reducing effects are well-known, acetaminophen actually weakens a person's ability to process positive emotions.[2]

Sevens have an insatiable desire for more pleasure but often deploy many pain-reducing strategies (most of which aren't as obvious as pills) that may lead to less pleasure and more pain. The lie Sevens believe is *it's not okay to feel pain,* which causes them to avoid pain at all costs. After eating the forbidden fruit and experiencing shame for the first time, Adam and Eve ran from God and sewed together fig leaves to cover the awful feeling. Sevens recapitulate this original shame-response, hiding their negative emotions from God—and, inevitably, from themselves. They sew fig leaves that say, "Don't worry, be happy!" to lighten things up and cover any sadness. They may skip grieving with the community on Good Friday to avoid facing the agony of Jesus' death, because for them, "every day is Easter." But when we keep the pain of the cross at bay, the joy of resurrection loses much of its power.

> Pain doesn't have to be the end of you; it can be the beginning of a new you.

Other fig leaf strategies include deflecting painful questions by telling others a story or perhaps by putting your feelings on the backburner altogether—until of course it starts a fire and forces your attention later on! You may also intellectualize your emotions by relabeling them as "stress" because that's easier to manage; or you might sugar-coat sad realities, putting a positive spin on painful memories to make others laugh when they should be crying with you.

Don't buy into the lie that what you don't see won't hurt you; keep an eye on the rearview mirror to face what you're running from before it catches up to you.

***The Good News for Enthusiasts*** is pain doesn't have to be the end of you; it can be the beginning of a new you. Like Adam and Eve, God mercifully pursues us and replaces our fragile fig leaves with better garments. Because of Christ's sacrifice, we won't be trapped in guilt or shame forever. But it's necessary to feel our emotions now so that we finally turn to God for help. In fact, the defining

---

2  Geoffrey R O Durso, Andrew Luttrell, and Baldwin M Way, "Over-the-Counter Relief From Pains and Pleasures Alike: Acetaminophen Blunts Evaluation Sensitivity to Both Negative and Positive Stimuli," Psychological science (U.S. National Library of Medicine, June 2015), https://www.ncbi.nlm.nih.gov/pmc/articles/PMC4515109/.

moment in a Seven's life is often when God allows you to experience a pain you can't outrun. To use C.S. Lewis' metaphor, pain is God's megaphone to show us what's wrong with the world and what's true about ourselves.

The teacher of Ecclesiastes affirms that God has ordained for us "a time to weep, and a time to laugh; a time to mourn, and a time to dance."[3] In fact, Jesus was called "a man of sorrows and acquainted with grief."[4] He was able to hold space for grief and give us more empathy and compassion. And on the cross, soldiers offered Jesus wine mixed with myrrh—a narcotic sedative used to numb the excruciating pain of crucifixion—He declined it, instead choosing to face His pain with a sober mind.[5]

In heaven, we will sing louder precisely because we've endured the pain of mourning and death in this life. The deeper the pain, the deeper the joy to come. Therefore, knowing all our tears will be wiped away, we will keep singing:

O Joy that seekest me through pain,
I cannot close my heart to thee;
I trace the rainbow through the rain,
And feel the promise is not vain,
That morn shall tearless be.

---

### → Pray

Father, I'm thankful Jesus didn't run from pain but faced it on the cross so that I might be free from the agony of fear, guilt, and shame forever. Don't let me live life on the run, trying to avoid the inevitable. Give me the confidence I need today to take off the fig leaves and trust that I will accomplish Your purposes in truly feeling pain.

---

3   Ecclesiastes 3:4

4   Isaiah 53:3

5   "The Wine Jesus Drank," Desiring God, May 27, 2010, https://www.desiringgod.org/articles/the-wine-jesus-drank.

# Day 13 Reflections:

**Describe a defining moment in your life when you couldn't run from pain any longer. How did God get you through it?**

**What fig-leaf strategy do you use the most to numb yourself or avoid pain (deflection, denial, avoidance, humor, sugar-coating, intellectualizing, etc.)?**

**Where might your pain be directing you next? How can you help others who are going through similar situations?**

---

### ➜ Respond

Create space to journal for 5 to 10 minutes about a painful emotion that keeps surfacing in your life. Write out your most honest thoughts and trust that God will hold you, not allowing you to feel trapped in despair.

# Mozart's Minor Key

*Not only that, but we rejoice in our sufferings, knowing that suffering produces*

*endurance, and endurance produces character, and character produces*

*hope, and hope does not put us to shame, because God's love has been*

*poured into our hearts through the Holy Spirit who has been given to us.*

—Romans 5:3-5

WOLFGANG AMADEUS MOZART WAS NOT THE SERIOUS, aging man many have in their heads but a hedonistic, impulsive young man who died at thirty-five. Though people have always taken his music seriously, those who knew him did not take him seriously. Mozart was infamous for inappropriate humor and frivolous behavior without regard for consequences.[1] Mozart's own sister, Maria Anna Mozart, shared, "This same being who, considered as an artist, had reached the highest stage of development even from his very earliest years, remained to the end of his life completely childish in every other aspect

> Most people want to grow, but the price of growth is pain.
>
> –Dan B. Allender

---

1 Harold C. Schonberg, *The Lives of the Great Composers* (New York: W.W. Norton, 1997).

of existence. Never, until he died, did he learn to exercise the most elementary forms of self-control."[2]

Mozart embodies many of the characteristics of an Enthusiast. Their sheer volume of creative output can be astounding, and their general playfulness is evident in all they do, such as Mozart's very Seven-ish opera, *The Marriage of Figaro*: a cheerful love-story filled with trickery, practical jokes, and humor.[3] But like unhealthy Sevens, Mozart was a pleasure-seeker who rarely confronted the darker side of life, for instance, only writing a few minor-key pieces and instead focusing on more uplifting or flighty tunes.

Average Sevens have the tendency to be a mile wide and an inch deep. Emotions like anger, sadness, fear, and disappointment are perceived to be a disease—get too close and you'll get infected. To put it another way, negative emotions are feared to be quicksand that will pull you under without any chance of escape. This leads Sevens to live off the lighter notes, perpetually playing their life's music in a major key. But this leaves them with only a half range of emotions, keeping their character and relationships shallow.[4] As such, Sevens are known to have a great *breadth* of relationships, but they struggle mightily to keep any with real depth.

To go deeper, Enneagram author Christian Wilcox suggests viewing the darker emotions of life not as a force that will overtake you but as the missing puzzle piece your life needs to be whole and complete.[5] Pain helps us to learn from our mistakes, teaches us how we still need to grow, reveals injustices, points out where we still need healing, and may even direct us toward our purpose and calling. Slowly processing these things will allow you to ripen like a green fruit to fuller and sweeter maturity and become someone who others take more seriously.

---

2   H.B. Stendhal, *The Lives of Haydn, Mozart & Metastasio* (London: Calder & Boyars, 1972).

3   "Mozart's Best Music: Where to Start with Mozart's Piano Concerto No. 21," Classic FM, accessed June 12, 2023, https://www.classicfm.com/composers/mozart/guides/mozarts-best-music-where-start/piano-concerto-21/.

4   Stabile, *The Path Between Us*, 167.

5   Christina S. Wilcox, *Take Care of Your Type: An Enneagram Guide to Self-Care* (New York, NY: Tiller Press, 2021), 141-142.

Shortly before Mozart's death, he was commissioned by a patron who had lost his young wife to an illness earlier that year. He struggled as he wrote "Requiem in D Minor," filled with fearful angst and an unwillingness to accept or deal with death. Mozart's wife claimed that he became convinced he was writing the piece for his own funeral. The intuition was right, as the genius died before it was finished. His musical legacy was brought to a close by this moving piece that helped one widow (and later the rest of the world) grapple with the mystery of death: "Requiem in D Minor" was chosen by the Catholic church to be played in their requiem mass in the centuries to follow. This minor-key masterpiece shows us the kind of legacy a Seven can have when they wrestle with their pain, allowing it to move through them and pour out into the world creatively.[6]

**The Good News for Enthusiasts** is "that if you let go of your wings and balloons, you won't fall into the tomb," as Dr. Jerry Wagner says.[7] The apostle Paul goes so far as to say we should find *joy* in our suffering. Why? Because we know "suffering produces endurance, and endurance produces character, and character produces hope."[8] When we finally accept pain is the price of growth, our character and all our relationships benefit. The psalmists reveal that the first step to being a man or woman after God's own heart is to play your minor notes—your pains, complaints, and heartaches—before God. As Jon Acuff says, "Wrestling with God is a sign of intimacy. You can't wrestle with someone you're far away from."

---

### → Pray

Father, I confess all the times I've wanted to tread on the surface or even stay on the shore—all to avoid life's dark waters. Give me more of the joy of the Holy Spirit, who can turn suffering into endurance. Help me play the music of the gospel for others, making sure to include both major and minor notes.

---

6   "Mozart's Requiem review – transcendent choral work returns with added poignancy," The Guardian, November 13, 2020, https://www.theguardian.com/music/2020/nov/13/mozart-requiem-choral-work-english-national-opera-coliseum-london-covid.

7   Wagner, *The Enneagram Spectrum of Personality Styles.*

8   Romans 5:3-4

# Day 14 Reflections:

**How have emotions like anger, sadness, fear, or disappointment grown your character and endurance?**

**What would change if you viewed darker emotions as the missing puzzle piece in your life?**

**When have you wrestled with God like the psalmists did? What was the outcome?**

---

**➜ Respond**

Choose a friend to go deeper with this week. Share more of your anxiety, sadness, or disappointments with them.

# Work Slashers

*Then I said to them, "You see the trouble we are in, how Jerusalem*

*lies in ruins with its gates burned. Come, let us build the wall*

*of Jerusalem, that we may no longer suffer derision."*

—Nehemiah 2:17

---

SEVENS ARE CLASSIC "SLASHERS." NO, I'M NOT talking about the creepy psychopaths stalking through a horror film with sharp objects. Marci Alboher, the author/journalist/speaker who popularized the term in his book *One Person/ Multiple Careers*, the word refers to the slash sign on the keyboard ("/") and points to a person with multiple jobs or roles (x/y/z/ etc.); someone who likes to combine roles or occupational identities and enjoys being in radically different, evolving environments.[2] My friend Elvin is a great example of a slasher, who is right now pastoring a new multiethnic

> God isn't offended by your biggest dreams or boldest prayers. He is offended by anything less.
>
> –Mark Batterson[1]

---

1   Mark Batterson, *The Circle Maker: Praying Circles Around Your Biggest Dreams and Greatest Fears* (United States: Zondervan, 2016), 15.

2   "What is a 'slasher'?" Programme Octave, accessed June 12, 2023, https://programmeoctave.com/en/6820/qui-sont-les-slasheurs/.

church he helped start, serving on the local board of Young Life, moonlighting as a comic in local clubs, and helping people buy and sell homes with his newly acquired realtor's license.

All Sevens are "activators": people who refuse to merely "pray about it," instead living by the motto, "The worst action is to take no action." One such biblical character was the fifth century BC Jewish deportee, Nehemiah, who supervised the rebuilding of Jerusalem. After hearing Jerusalem's walls were broken down and its gates destroyed by fire, he sat and wept for days—praying and fasting. Rather than waiting for God to send someone else, Nehemiah realized God wanted him to be the answer to his own prayer. With the Babylonian Emperor's approval, Nehemiah traveled to Jerusalem, secretly surveyed the rubble, and determined the size and scope of the project. Then, like a persuasive Seven, this cup-bearer/activist/construction foreman got further permission from the emperor to rebuild.[3]

Sevens bring show-stopping strengths to their work. These best-case scenario thinkers have an optimistic, positive attitude that makes work fun and lifts everyone's spirits. They are enthusiastic supporters who celebrate individual and team victories, and though they prefer to do things their way, they are great listeners who will adapt to make others feel heard and supported. Making friends with nearly everyone and being extremely likable, these humorous and charming co-workers enjoy planning social gatherings for the team. These fun co-workers are also innovative, forward-thinking planners, and fast-paced doers who don't get bogged down by problems but find solutions. They are master ideators who know how to brainstorm new opportunities and ways of doing things for the company.[4]

> Sevens are master ideators who know how to brainstorm new opportunities and ways of doing things.

To thrive in the workplace, Sevens need a fast-paced, creative, flexible environment with a heavy dose of independence and a long leash. They are fantastic team players who need a multifaceted job description that allows

---

3   Nehemiah 1:3–2:8

4   Chestnut, *The 9 Types of Leadership*, 229-230.

them to multitask a variety of things at once. Their sweet spot is getting on a whiteboard, planning for the future, synthesizing complex information, and communicating it with simplicity. They get short-term projects off the ground, acquire resources, and energize teams to make it all happen by tomorrow (or ideally, by yesterday).

However, they *aren't* typically great at managing and maintaining people and projects—details are definitely not their forté. Also, they often need help with professional decision-making because there are too many options, and all of them sound good. When presented with two choices, the classic Seven response is "Why not both?" They make great team leaders—until the weight of responsibility becomes too much or their new start-up grows and people start making demands for more processes and structure. At that point, it may be best to hand the baton to someone else and find a new trail to blaze.[5]

***The Good News for Enthusiasts*** is, though Nehemiah felt trapped and limited working in the King's court, God opened a door to a new opportunity that would change the Jewish nation forever. Because Nehemiah didn't just "pray about it" but also got to work, he paved the way for the Messiah's triumphal entry into Jerusalem. Like Nehemiah, God will use you to do things that seem impossible. But you must not act too quickly on your brilliant ideas (something a Seven is prone to do); slow down to pray and fast like Nehemiah first. Then and only then will you be able to look back and say "for the good hand of my God was upon me."[6]

---

**→ Pray**

Father, thank You for giving me incredible gifts and abilities. Like Nehemiah, I know that if I ask anything in Your name You'll make it happen.[7] Help me to keep praying big, bold prayers as I dream about best-case scenarios. Slow me down enough today to listen to Your voice. I know if I acknowledge You first, my paths will be straight.[?]

---

5   Ian Morgan Cron and Suzanne Stabile, *The Road Back to You* (Downers Grove, IL: InterVarsity Press Books, 2016), 221-222.

6   Nehemiah 2:8

7   John 16:23

# Day 15 Reflections:

**Which of the workplace strengths do you see most in yourself? Please explain.**

**What do you need in your workplace to thrive? Have you communicated these to your boss?**

**How can you prioritize prayer and fasting over taking action?**

> ### → Respond
>
> Write down a seemingly impossible project you would like your team to accomplish if you knew God's hand was on you. Then rally the troops to pray, fast, and run after it.

# Blind Spots at Work

*Everyone then who hears these words of mine and does them will be*

*like a wise man who built his house on the rock. And the rain fell,*

*and the floods came, and the winds blew and beat on that house,*

*but it did not fall, because it had been founded on the rock.*

—Matthew 7:24-25

ENTHUSIASTS CAN REALLY STRUGGLE WHEN THEIR WORKPLACE culture doesn't value trust, freedom, and movement. Sevens strive to move their organizations into the future, but hierarchies, bureaucracies, institutional structures, and other measures that are put in place to control people and outcomes just seem to slow everything down. Don't try to micromanage a Seven, reduce their budget, or trap them in a boring role unless you want to get into a verbal sparring match with them … and lose. A Seven's "hell" is being stuck in a cubicle, controlled by a by-the-book boss who leads an unenthusiastic team in a status-quo organization. No

> If you obey all the rules you miss all the fun.
>
> –Katharine Hepburn[1]

1   Tracy Tresidder, Margaret Loftus, and Jacqui Pollock, *Knowing Me, Knowing Them: Understand Your Parenting Personality by Discovering the Enneagram* (Carlton North, Victoria, Australia: Monterey Press, 2014), 126-127.

surprise we find Sevens jumping from one career to another, or opting out of organizations entirely and being self-employed.

As we discussed yesterday, Sevens bring many strengths to the workplace, yet like the rest of us, they can struggle when their strengths are overdone: in this case their quick thinking, fast pivoting, and need for speed can lead others into frustration and eventually, confrontation. There's no time for routine paperwork, repetitive tasks, or getting bogged down by feelings for these dynamos! As Beatrice Chestnut shares, coworkers of unhealthy Sevens have said these fun-loving, distractible leaders can be hard to talk to when they are going through a rough time because of a perceived lack of depth. Other examples include Sevens not having the fortitude to work through relational issues, not being able to focus on or complete projects that aren't "fun," not following through on their commitments, and exhausting others while running after the latest idea.[2]

> Your presence is more important than what you produce.

Other blind spots in the workplace that Sevens need to be aware of, according to Chestnut, are seeing things through rose-colored glasses and overlooking the negative data (one Seven-pastor I know says that denial is his "drug of choice"), rationalizing away bad results, or getting so lost in their imagined utopian world that they lose touch with reality. They may skim along the surface of things rather than doing more research or paying attention to the details, or celebrate too quickly before goals are actually reached.[3]

Sevens may also get into conflict with their bosses when they start bending the rules or running outside of their lane—leaving their managers to feel like the "bad guys" for having to place common sense limits on them. In general, Sevens tend to have an anti-authoritarian stance and seek to flatten the hierarchy so that they can't be controlled and so that everyone on the team feels like equals. They generally are great friends with those above them and below them on the totem pole.

---

2  Chestnut, *The 9 Types of Leadership*, 239.

3  Ibid., 229.

I tell my Seven friends all the time: Your *presence* is more important than what you *produce*. You have a way of lifting the entire room as you cheer us on and throw yourself into the work, with all of its challenges, maintaining a positive attitude and expecting us to win. When the work is draining and hard times come, it will be less painful because you are in the room with us.

One last thing that needs to be said is that it's particularly difficult to be a female Seven in our culture. My friend Abby shared that, because of the long-standing patriarchal expectations of women to be administrative or helpers, they are not always well-received as thought-leaders or driven entrepreneurs. Much like female Eights, they get very frustrated when others perceive their healthy pushback as criticism or complaining (though the same traits are praised as bold leadership when done by men).

**The Good News for Enthusiasts** is that your work will be successful if you don't build your house on your grand plans but on the solid rock of God's wisdom. A foolish man who builds his career on constantly-shifting sand is one who works hastily and impatiently on many castles that end up getting blown over or washed up. But the wise man listens to God's wisdom and works patiently and thoughtfully, always counting the cost and enjoying God's presence throughout the process. If you do this, not only will your future be secure, but those next to you will be smiling rather than catching their breath!

---

### → Pray

Father, I know You created work to be fun and that the thorns and thistles we experience as a result of the curse of sin will one day be undone.[4] Give me more mercy for the serious types who seem to enjoy making more work and help me to pay more attention to my blind spots so that I can experience greater fruitfulness and joy in my daily tasks.

---

4  Genesis 3:17-19

# Day 16 Reflections:

**Which personal value or leadership style of yours seems to conflict the most with the Western workplace? How have you navigated this difference?**

**When has your need for novelty, change, freedom, or a fast pace negatively impacted your managers or co-workers?**

**What is your biggest takeaway from today's reading?**

> **→ Respond**
>
> Because that brilliant mind of yours is a fast processor, others may feel anxious at times when you have no filter. One tip is to be mindful in conversation and talk 50 percent slower and 50 percent less to create more space for others to respond to you and participate more.

# Squirrel!

*[Jesus] said, "Follow me." But he said, "Lord, let me first go and bury my father." And Jesus said to him, "Leave the dead to bury their own dead. But as for you, go and proclaim the kingdom of God." Yet another said, "I will follow you, Lord, but let me first say farewell to those at my home." Jesus said to him, "No one who puts his hand to the plow and looks back is fit for the kingdom of God."*

—Luke 9:59-62

---

DISNEY AND PIXAR'S *UP* IS A MUST-SEE film for all Enthusiasts, according to my friend John Fooshee. In this heartwarming, tear-jerking, hilarious adventure, the main characters, Carl and Russel, meet a wacky, talking dog named Doug, who helps them on their journey. However, Doug and his canine friends have one Achilles heel: squirrels. It doesn't matter what is happening at the moment or how much danger is involved, when a squirrel appears, the dogs' attention is immediately redirected.

> The most dangerous distractions are the ones you love, but that don't love you back.
>
> —Warren Buffett

Have you ever set out to accomplish a task only to experience Shiny Squirrel

Syndrome just one minute later? Part of the problem is that freakishly brilliant mind of yours, overflowing in real-time with creative ideas that don't seem to stop. Additionally, Sevens often have excellent memories that absorb stories, movie lines, and other random facts like light on a strip of film.[1] But a problem occurs when your "beautiful mind" turns into "monkey mind" and you begin rapidly switching from one thing to another until your train of thought runs off the tracks.

While a daily adventure of twists and turns may sound fun, this "pinball machine lifestyle" of bouncing from one task or person to the next will eventually take all your change. The apostle Paul told Timothy he must instruct the church to resist the busybody syndrome. Busybodies, while always having something to do, are rarely occupied with the things they should (and actually want) to be doing.

> Give the world a well-cooked feast rather than a half-baked buffet.

Today's passage highlights the tension of desiring to stay focused on the main thing amid everyday life. One man asked to stay and "bury [his] father," which sounds reasonable, but that phrase doesn't mean his father was already dead. Rather, his request was to remain with his aging father until he passed, which could delay discipleship indefinitely. Jesus challenged the man to not let that excuse become a distraction from fulfilling his higher purpose of proclaiming the kingdom of God.

Do you find it challenging to postpone fun ideas? To not procrastinate or be redirected and instead take an important project all the way to the finish line? Has your lack of focus or discipline led you to spread yourself too thin, forget details, or miss appointments? Then follow the apostle Paul's example: "So I do not run aimlessly; I do not box as one beating the air. But I discipline my body and keep it under control."[2] Okay now, that's easy for *you* to say, Paul—disciplined Type One that you are![3] Truly, as Sevens grow, they learn from and adopt the diligence,

---

1   Don Riso and Russ Hudson, *Personality Types: Using the Enneagram for Self-Discovery* (New York, NY: Houghton Mifflin Company Books, 1996), 269.

2   1 Corinthians 9:26-27

3   My hunch is that Paul is the One-to-one subtype of Type One which outwardly appears like a Type Eight.

discipline, responsibility, and accountability of healthy Type Ones. Observe their ways! Watch how they sacrifice their selfish desires, set realistic deadlines, and implement their ideas. (Don't worry, I already told them in their devotional book how to loosen up and enjoy life more like you!)

While you're at it, you would also do well to study the ways of Type Fives, which is another growth path for Sevens. Create more space for solitude so you can be more thoughtful about your ideas and increase your level of quality and execution. Another tip is to finish your tasks before moving on to the next one—like that house project you've been working on (or this amazing book you are reading right now). Finally, try doing the hardest task on your to-do list first to get it out of the way. You may find that it only takes five minutes to complete a task you've been avoiding for five months.

***The Good News for Enthusiasts*** is that though it may feel impossible becoming someone who can avoid chasing the squirrels, one of the fruits of the Holy Spirit is *self-control*.[4] While exercising self-control might come more naturally to some people, I know it's a real struggle for you. But God promises to give you the Holy Spirit's power to become more focused, thorough, and methodical as you take only the right ideas at the right time and cook them to completion to give the world a well-cooked feast rather than a half-baked buffet.

---

### → Pray

Father, I get distracted by many things. It's hard to stay focused on what's most important. But when I look at Your Son, Jesus, I see a Man with focus. He had to tell people no so often to stay on task and show love to many. He filtered everything through loving You and loving people. Give me that same focus. Tell me what I am to do next. I'm listening.

---

4  Galatians 5:22-23

# Day 17 Reflections:

**What are the "squirrels" that distract you the most? How can you eliminate them?**

**How has procrastination affected your life and relationships?**

**When are you going to do that important task God or others keep asking you to do but you keep avoiding?**

## → Respond

Use the Eisenhower matrix to prioritize your tasks into these four quadrants: urgent and important (do first), not urgent but important (schedule), urgent and not-important (delegate), and not urgent and not important (don't do).[5]

---

5   "Eisenhower Matrix," Eisenhower.me, accessed June 12, 2023, https://www.eisenhower.me/eisenhower-matrix/.

# Grass Is Greener

*And as he sowed, some seeds fell along the path, and the birds*

*came and devoured them. Other seeds fell on rocky ground, where*

*they did not have much soil, and immediately they sprang up,*

*since they had no depth of soil, but when the sun rose they were*

*scorched. And since they had no root, they withered away.*

—Matthew 13:4-6

MY WIFE, LINDSEY, AND I TRY TO take a couples trip to a new city every year, and one of our favorite destinations has been San Francisco. After walking the city for a week, we hopped in our rental car and traveled north to Muir Woods, a large redwood forest where some of the trees reach 250 feet high and 30 feet in diameter! While I had seen images of these magnificent giants of nature before, standing next to them was an entirely different experience.

> The grass is greener wherever you water it.
>
> —Neil Barringham[1]

Walking through the forest, it was hard for us to comprehend that some of these were

1   Jay Shetty, *Think Like a Monk: Train Your Mind for Peace and Purpose Every Day* (New York, NW: Simon & Schuster, 2020), 35.

mere sprouting seeds over 2,000 years ago when Jesus walked the earth. How does something so big come from something so small, and how does it survive so long? Every seed, though it's not immediately apparent, has the imprint of something much bigger within it. The same is true of you: God has imprinted the divine image on your soul, and though your faith may begin smaller than a redwood seed, it has the potential to grow into something truly magnificent. You were not created to be a small, solitary house plant but a giant redwood that can weather endless storms rooted in the life of your community.

Unfortunately, a "grass is greener" mentality keeps Sevens from obtaining this lofty vision. Just as in gardening, transplanting is necessary in life sometimes too; that is, moving to a healthier relationship, community, church, or workplace to provide you with richer soil to thrive in. Keep in mind, though, that continually transplanting yourself to seemingly greener pastures will keep your roots thin and shallow. In the parable of the sower, Jesus explained some people hear the Word and immediately receive it with joy. They spring up quickly and rather impressively but fail to keep growing because their shallow roots couldn't endure the heat of the sun.

> Continually transplanting yourself to seemingly greener pastures will keep your roots thin and shallow.

When Sevens get intrigued by what's on the other side of the fence, a new idea may become a "new calling."[2] Instead of dipping their toes in the water, they will dive in the deep end and abandon what they are currently doing, not only stunting their own growth but also depriving their old community of their presence. After all, redwoods famously have a shallow root system—they have stood for centuries by interlocking their roots, by holding each other. For the unhealthy (flighty) Seven, once that new calling becomes old, boring, or the adrenaline wears off, it's time to move on. More than any other Enneagram type, Sevens have a fear of missing out when it comes to big things like their

---

2  Wilcox, *Take Care of Your Type*, 131-132.

career path or even small things like everyday conversations. FOMO is always crouching at your door, but you must not let it control your life.[3]

***The Good News for Enthusiasts*** is the grass will be greener right where you are if you stick around to water it. The Prodigal Son had everything he ever needed, his father's love and presence, right where he was. However, a grass is greener mentality transplanted him to a distant land; that is, until his green grass turned into mud. Thankfully, no matter how many times you wander from home, a loving Father will be right there waiting for you with open arms.[4] He's ready to free you from the tiring treadmill of having to chase the next thing on your bucket list to *finally* feel satisfied.

Before you start dreaming about a distant land, give your current idea, relationship, home, community, hobby, or role more time to develop to see if it's meant to be. Let the roots grow a little more. Typically, Sevens don't stay with what they have long enough to see any fruit grow on the tree after all their labor. Therefore, decide right now what you want to stick with for the foreseeable future and how you'll battle the waves of discontentment when they come. Use your imagination right now to forecast both the mountains *and* valleys you'll experience in the journey ahead, remembering that the mountaintop experiences will be that much brighter after walking in the dark.

---

### ➜ Pray

Father, I bless Your holy name! You have forgiven my sins and redeemed my life from the pit. Your Son, Jesus, received a crown of thorns so that I would be crowned with Your steadfast love and mercy. By Your Holy Spirit, help me to never forget all You've done for me. Enable me to lead a celebratory life that rejoices in You always.

---

3   Genesis 4:7 NIV

4   Luke 15:11-32

# Day 18 Reflections:

**Describe one long-term commitment you've followed through on. What would you have missed out on if you would've given up too soon?**

**Why is the joy of lived experience more satisfying than the temporary pursuit of enjoyment?**

**What roots do you need to nurture and let grow a little more to see long-lasting fruit?**

### ➥ Respond

Start a garden in the backyard or a collection of plants in your home. The process of daily nurturing your plants and waiting patiently for them to grow will help discipline you to go against the grain of quick hits of excitement.[5]

---

5    Drew Moser, *The Enneagram of Discernment: The Way of Vocation, Wisdom, and Practice* (Beaver Falls, PA: Falls City Press, 2020), 365.

# Blind Spots in Love

*Love is patient and kind; love does not envy or boast; it is not arrogant*

*or rude. It does not insist on its own way; it is not irritable or resentful;*

*it does not rejoice at wrongdoing, but rejoices with the truth. Love bears*

*all things, believes all things, hopes all things, endures all things.*

—1 Corinthians 13:4-7

ENTHUSIASTS IN LOVE MAKE LIFE-LONG COMPANIONS WHO find adventure behind every corner of life—and long to share these with their partner. Sevens are often misunderstood in relationships because their excitement to implement a new idea can come off as controlling, their natural assertiveness as argumentative, and their natural charisma as flirtatious even when they aren't trying to be.

> Oh darling, let's be adventurers.
>
> –Anonymous

Sevens want to be with someone who gives them freedom while keeping them grounded in life.[1] Suzanne Stabile shares one of the greatest struggles for Sevens in relationships: "Every Seven I know has a big heart: they are

---

1 Stephanie Barron Hall, *The Enneagram in Love: A Roadmap for Building and Strengthening Romantic Relationships* (Emeryville, CA: Rockridge Press, 2020), 67.

generous and willing to make sacrifices for those they love. But more than any other number I think they feel trapped, caught between their seemingly endless need for stimulation and the needs of others. Listen closely and you will hear a lot of Sevens say, 'I want to do whatever it takes for you to be happy.' And they mean it, but they don't want to lose themselves in the process."[2]

Today, we'll look at some of the blind spots these life- and love-loving adventurers have in relationships. Though it won't be easy, the heart behind this is to help you improve relationships, avoid unnecessary pain, and prevent any surprises in the future. For guidance, let's turn to 1 Corinthians 13:4-7 and read the apostle Paul's classic chapter on love in his first letter to the Corinthian church.

*Love is not arrogant.* Sevens must resist the temptation to blame others, instead taking full responsibility for their part in conflict.[3]

*Love is not rude.* It does not look like dominating the conversation, failing to show up with empathy when others want to share the harder aspects of life, or neglecting your responsibilities and leaving them for another. It does not drop your plans with someone at the last minute because you found something more fun to do, nor does it string someone along while you remain uncommitted.[4]

> Sevens may prioritize the pursuit of pleasure over the object of their love.

*Love does not insist on its own way.* It does not pester others to do what you want, prioritizing your needs over theirs. It does not move too fast and furious, exhausting loved ones in the process.

*Love bears all things and endures all things.* Average Sevens may prioritize the pursuit of pleasure over the object of their love. The thrill of "the chase," a bucket-list date, or physical intimacy may get confused as true love. And when the adventure of being in love becomes an end in itself, unhealthy Sevens will bounce from one relationship to the next, skating over opportunities to take it

---

2   Stabile, *The Path Between Us*, 169.

3   Ibid., 168.

4   Sarajane Case, *The Honest Enneagram: Know Your Type, Own Your Challenges, Embrace Your Growth* (Kansas City, MO: Andrews McMeel Publishing, 2020), 181.

deeper. To keep things romantic or positive, they may idealize the other person and choose not to look at their flaws until it's no longer possible—at which point they may drop them on a dime without any warning or guilt.

These blind spots are general for Sevens and may not apply to you, but either way, they aren't fun to hear, so let me remind you how much we appreciate you: your enthusiasm is life-giving, and your positivity helps us stay focused on the praiseworthy aspects of life. You help us to experience life to its fullest. We feel deeply connected when you sit with us and plan out a bright future together. Life is hard, but your humor and sense of adventure makes it lighter. Relationships are hard, but your ability to see the good in us smooths conflicts over because your love *believes all things and hopes all things.* All that to say, there ain't no sunshine when you're gone.

***The Good News for Enthusiasts*** is that in the light of Jesus' life of sacrificial love, we can see our blind spots clearly. Through Jesus, the multi-faceted love of the triune Godhead described in 1 Corinthians 13 has been made visible to us. Just as a diverse spectrum of bright colors shine through a crystal prism, so too do the patience, kindness, truth, and enduring love of the Father shine through the Son with magnificent glory. If you have seen and tasted this radiant love, go and love others in the same way today.

---

### → Pray

Father, You have loved me so well. When it comes to loving others selflessly, my love sometimes falls short. Help me not to insist on having my way all the time and show my loved ones they are my number one priority. Enable me by Your Holy Spirit to offer others empathy from the well of Your steadfast love, which endures forever.

---

# Day 19 Reflections:

**How have you demonstrated God's love through your positivity, sense of adventure, and seeing the best in others?**

**When has your fear of boredom, limitations, negative feelings, or long-term commitment hurt your relationships?**

**Which blind spot do you struggle with the most? What can you do about it?**

---

### ➦ Respond

Because average Sevens are self-referencing, try and catch yourself today putting too much attention on what *you* want and need. Notice how this tendency can lead you to lack empathy or offer support for your loved ones.[5]

---

5    Beatrice Chestnut and Uranio Paes, *The Enneagram Guide to Waking Up: Find Your Path, Face Your Shadow, Discover Your True Self* (Charlottesville, VA: Hampton Roads Publishing, 2021), 186-187.

# Cup of Suffering

*"Father, if you are willing, remove this cup from me. Nevertheless, not my will, but yours, be done." And there appeared to him an angel from heaven, strengthening him. And being in agony he prayed more earnestly; and his sweat became like great drops of blood falling down to the ground.*

—Luke 22:42-44

You probably have a mental list of things you don't want to happen in life—getting rebuked by Jesus is probably one of them. Unfortunately for the apostle Peter, he experienced this in such a memorable and public way that we still read about it two thousand years later. Resisting Jesus' intimations of future suffering and death, Peter pushed back, only to hear his Rabbi retort, "Get behind me, Satan!" Why was Jesus so harsh? Because Peter actively resisted the idea of a Suffering Savior.[2]

> Face your life,
>
> Its pain, its pleasure,
>
> Leave no path untaken.
>
> —Neil Gaiman[1]

---

1  Tara Prescott and Neil Gaiman, *Neil Gaiman in the 21st Century Essays on the Novels, Children's Stories, Online Writings, Comics and Other Works* (Jefferson, NC: McFarland & Company, Inc. Publishers, 2015), 93.

2  Mark 8:31-33

Similarly, average Enthusiasts have a robust theology of *resurrection* but an anemic theology of suffering. They want to celebrate Easter, but not Good Friday, which is why I think Jesus' prayer in the garden of Gethsemane on the night He was betrayed is one of the most important scenes in the Bible for Sevens. God the Son, being fully human, experienced the same fear and anxiety that we do—but to the nth degree. While praying intensely, body trembling, and sweating profusely (even drawing blood), He asked the Father to "remove this cup from me." Perhaps there was another way to bring about the redemption of the world without such pain? But in the end, Jesus said, "Not my will, but yours, be done."[3]

The average Enthusiast would rather grab a red Solo cup than the one Jesus received, but make no mistake: the well-aged wine is coming, and we can already smell the feast cooking in heaven's kitchen. There's just a little more progress for us pilgrims left in this world to make before that day comes. In this case, repentance for a Seven looks like exchanging your version of the Christian life for one that includes pain. In other words, you "take up [your] cross"[4] to follow Jesus on the road marked with suffering rather than seeking to go around it.

The only way out of suffering is through it—there are no shortcuts.

The day of reckoning for a Seven comes when you finally face a painful trial too big to run from.[5] Perhaps it's a relationship break-up, the loss of a job, a medical diagnosis, infertility, a miscarriage, or saying good-bye to a loved one. These are the sort of situations that will force you to slow down and confront your pain head on if you are even the least bit aware and open. The decision you have to make is whether you'll take the cup and walk directly *through* the suffering, or continue trying to find ways to evade it. Remember, the only way out of suffering is through it—there are no shortcuts.

Ian Cron shares some great advice to Sevens: "No one can manufacture optimism continuously without sacrificing a part of their humanity. Life's challenges are

---

3 Luke 22:42

4 Luke 9:23

5 Liz Carver and Josh Green, *What's Your Enneatype?: Understanding the Nine Personality Types for Personal Growth and Strengthened Relationships* (Beverly, MA: Fair Winds Press, an imprint of The Quarto Group, 2020).

unavoidable and produce seasons of loss, disappointment, and wounding. Just because they're not acknowledged and owned doesn't mean that you ducked life's punches. Sevens prefer to suffer privately rather than letting anyone else see them bleed, especially themselves. In order for healing to ever occur, there needs to be a time of feeling the pain, dressing the wounds, and allowing scars to form."[6]

An unattended emotional wound will continue to tear open and swell within. Scars, however, are not wounds, but are a visible reminder you have survived and experienced God's healing. Then you can show others the results of pain faced head-on.

***The Good News for Enthusiasts*** is that just as the prophet Isaiah predicted, the Messiah came and was "crushed for our iniquities"—those we have done and have been done to us—so that by "his wounds we are healed."[7] When healed and healthy, Sevens become the perfect examples of how to endure suffering well. When hardships come their way, they don't play the victim but bounce back quickly. They model the Phoenix, allowing pain to do its healing work, so they might rise from the ashes. Though they've been through the worst circumstances, they keep going with smiles on their faces—not smiles of blissful, ignorant denial, but of the confidence of One who has died and risen to new life.

---

### → Pray

Father, thank You for showing me through Your Son, Jesus, that suffering will not be the end of me. Help me by the Spirit's power not to run from pain but develop the fortitude to face life's adversity. In solidarity with my Suffering Savior, I will take up my cross and choose the road marked with suffering, knowing greater joy waits on the other side.

---

6   Cron, *The Story of You*, 179-180.

7   Isaiah 53:5

# Day 20 Reflections:

**What have you survived or been healed of by God's grace?**

**Like Peter, how have you resisted a theology of suffering? What is an unpleasant part of life you need to embrace rather than go around?**

**Where are there still open emotional or spiritual wounds that need your attention? Invite Jesus to bring healing to those parts of your heart.**

---

### ➜ Respond

Plan a time to share about one of your "healed scars" to give others hope that God can show up in their suffering.

# The Vice of Gluttony

*Jesus said to her, "Everyone who drinks of this water will be thirsty again,*

*but whoever drinks of the water that I will give him will never be thirsty*

*again. The water that I will give him will become in him a spring of water*

*welling up to eternal life." The woman said to him, "Sir, give me this*

*water, so that I will not be thirsty or have to come here to draw water."*

—John 4:13-15

---

ROCK AND ROLL LEGENDS U2 WERE ONCE members of a Christian fellowship in their native Ireland called *Shalom*. As the band became more well known, they wondered if they should be doing something more meaningful than playing music—especially back then, when rock and roll seemed at odds with their Christian faith. But their manager pressured them to stick with it and well, the rest is history. U2's hit "I Still Haven't Found What I'm Looking For" was released in 1987, a song that lead singer Bono

> When choosing between two evils, I always like to take the one I've never tried before.
>
> —Mae West[1]

---

1    Wagele, *The Enneagram for Teens.*

referred to as "a gospel song with a restless spirit."[2] Fans across generations and continents have resonated with its authentic message because it taps into our real life experiences: the waiting, wanting, and searching.

The life of an Enthusiast is marked by a longing for *more*. Though the average Seven may look like Indiana Jones searching for the Holy Grail or Nicholas Cage tracking down the national treasure, they still haven't found what they're looking for. Unlike Type Fours, who find meaning in the hunger for more itself (and secretly hope it will never be satisfied!), Sevens are desperately hoping the next thing will fill the void.

The deadly sin, or vice, of the Seven is *gluttony*: with eyes bigger than their stomachs, Enthusiasts' spiritual appetite leads them to try everything to satiate the need. In this sense, gluttony could mean consuming large portions of food, but it also includes filling an insatiable appetite with stimulating ideas, sexual encounters, new relationships, travel plans, or upgrading your home or possessions—but it will never be enough. I am reminded of a fraternity brother of mine who always cracked the best jokes and seemed to be the life of the party; yet to everyone's surprise, he quit school and moved back home after falling into a deep state of depression.

Unhealthy Sevens are constantly filling themselves up but rarely feel full—like the feeling we got as kids when eating cotton candy. Sandra Maitri explains that "consuming rather than digesting is the focus" of gluttony.[3] When you consume something but don't digest it, you are left hungrier than before, like an addict who needs another "fix" to maintain an artificial high.

We are not what we devour but what we digest. Without slowing down to taste, smell, see, listen, or touch the gifts God gives us, we can't be satisfied. To find this peace and wholeness requires a "less is more" lifestyle that feels counterproductive in our world—especially to the average Seven. But when you

---

2   Elizabeth Blair, "In U2's 'I Still Haven't Found What I'm Looking For,' A Restless Search For Meaning," NPR, July 26, 2019, https://www.npr.org/2019/07/26/743620996/u2-i-still-havent-found-what-im-looking-for-american-anthem.

3   Chestnut, *The Complete Enneagram*.

experience the satisfaction of feeling spiritually full and the peace that follows, you will soon realize an indulgent life is not the same as a happy life.

**The Good News for Enthusiasts** is found in John 4, where we read about a woman who was perpetually searching for more. She maintained the fantasy that a relationship could bring peace and security and fill the void and emptiness. But even after five partners, she thirsted for something more filling. Then she met Jesus one day by a well. With eyes of loving-kindness, He offered her an eternal spring of intimate fulfillment that no partner could provide. Through this story, we learn that we *can* pile all of the deepest longings of our hearts onto one Person to quench our soul's deep spiritual thirst.

Like the woman at the well, Jesus graciously challenges you today to reflect on your recent search for happiness. Today, rather than attempting another "hail mary" at the next promise of fulfillment, follow the psalmist's counsel and "Delight yourself in the LORD, and he will give you the desires of your heart."[4] You may just find that the things you wanted were nothing like what you actually needed. My friend and Type Seven, Chris, said one of the most meaningful verses in the Bible for him is the story of the man who hid the treasure in a field and then with *joy* went and sold everything he had to buy the field.[5] Like Chris, you can let go of everything you *want* when you realize Christ is all that you need.

---

### → Pray

Father, forgive me for going to broken cisterns instead of You, my spring of living water.[6] As Your beloved child, remind me that I already have everything I need in Christ. Thank You for giving me the desires of my new heart. I will be satisfied every morning with Your steadfast love and will rejoice and be glad all the days of my life.[7]

---

4   Psalm 37:4

5   Matthew 13:44

6   Jeremiah 2:13

7   Psalm 90:14

# Day 21 Reflections:

**When have you seen the insatiable appetite for more show up in your life?**

**What has God done to satisfy you in a way the world never could?**

**How can you prevent unhealthy cravings by limiting overstimulation from technology or other experiences?**

---

**→ Respond**

Because gluttony triggers excitement, the next time you get excited about something, practice the discipline of stillness to reflect on where the craving is coming from.[8]

---

8    Chestnut and Paes, *The Enneagram Guide to Waking Up*, 196-197.

# The Virtue of Sobriety

*"Therefore I tell you, do not be anxious about your life, what you will eat or what you will drink, nor about your body, what you will put on. Is not life more than food, and the body more than clothing? Look at the birds of the air: they neither sow nor reap nor gather into barns, and yet your heavenly Father feeds them. Are you not of more value than they?"*

—Matthew 6:25-26

---

IN A SMALL PLAINS TOWN OF NEBRASKA, I grew up under the shadow of Saint Francis of Assisi. Raised a devout Catholic, I received my K-12 education at a school named after the poor saint, where my mother was a school teacher and my father was the President of the Catholic fraternal organization known as the Knights of Columbus. While the other boys in my grade school classes wanted to be firefighters and astronauts, this Type Three earned medals for outstanding service as an altar boy and wanted to be a priest.

> You have made us for yourself, O Lord, and our heart is restless until it rests in you.
>
> –St. Augustine

Ironically, I did enter the ministry as a Protestant pastor, but only after living up the "college life" for a few years. Turns out, this very same saint, whose statue adorned my childhood bedroom, did the same. The son of a wealthy merchant, Francis' exuberant love of life led him to become a "pleasure-seeking party king"[1] who had many serious moral lapses in his youth. But around the age of twenty, he became embroiled in the wars between his Italian city state, Assisi, and its neighbor, Perugia. During the war he was held prisoner for almost a year, becoming seriously ill at one point. After this season of reckoning, as well as family upheaval, Francis dedicated himself to solitude and prayer, resulting in his taking a vow of poverty.[2]

Francis' life is the perfect case study of someone who moved from the vice of *gluttony* to the virtue of *sobriety*. Within the Enneagram context, sobriety does not only mean freedom from alcohol but all intoxicating influences; it is living with *balance*: choosing quality over quantity, just the right amount over excess, and being present for *this one thing (whatever it may be)* over the many possible things.

> Sobriety means living a balanced life.

When writing to the fledgling churches of Asia Minor and hoping to inspire growth and strong leadership, the apostle Paul exhorted the communities to choose leaders who were "sober-minded,"[3] which is the ability to make decisions with a clear mind, free from any influences that may cloud their judgment. Similarly, Sevens must be able to rise above the addiction to pleasure so they can judge truth from error and reality from fantasy. Being sober-minded will help you become a more discerning leader, useful to others for your wisdom, not just your zeal.

Sobriety means living a balanced life rather than swinging on the pendulum of extremes (for example, learning how to be honest without being blunt or taking on a new hobby without getting obsessed). Balance also looks like living with a "healthy amount" of everything, taking only what you need in the moment.

---

1   Richard Rohr and Andreas Ebert, *The Enneagram: A Christian Perspective* (New York, NY: The Crossroad Publishing Company, 2001), 160-161.

2   "Saint Francis of Assisi," Britannica, April 24, 2023, https://www.britannica.com/biography/Saint-Francis-of-Assisi.

3   1 Peter 5:8

Francis, known as a lover of animals who even preached to the birds and beasts, learned contentment from them as he observed how they only gathered what they needed from hour to hour.[4]

Being sober also means detaching yourself from all the ideas occupying real estate in your head and practicing the art of being fully present. This requires you to learn how to say no more so that you can say yes to the richness of whatever or whoever is in front of you. When you say no and let go of your FOMO, you are really saying yes to JOMO—to the *joy* that accompanies missing out on some things to be here now for *this* thing. From here on out, take a minimalist approach to your time management, and choose meaningful experiences over meaningless highs. Remember, less is more.

***The Good News for Enthusiasts*** is Jesus commands you to "not be anxious about your life,"[5] because your heavenly Father takes care of you, just like the birds of the air who don't worry about what they'll eat or drink an hour from now. Rather, seize each moment as the divine gift that it is, taking pleasure in all the things you don't get to do in order to find joy in those things, people, and experiences that are here before you today.

Another great saint who spent his youth pursuing the path of the prodigal, Augustine, later testified, "You have made us for yourself, O Lord, and our heart is restless until it rests in you."

---

### → Pray

Father, I want to live a life of balance. Help me cultivate the virtue of sobriety with the help of the Holy Spirit. Though it feels like a paradox to me, show me, like You did for Francis and Augustine, how living a life of radical openness leads to greater joy. Because You take care of all my needs, I will be restfully present with whomever You lead me to today, ready and open to be Your presence in their lives.

---

4   "Did You Know St. Francis Had a Least Favorite Animal?" Aleteia, August 2, 2019, https://aleteia.org/2019/08/02/did-you-know-st-francis-had-a-least-favorite-animal/.

5   Matthew 6:25

# Day 22 Reflections:

**When was the last time you were fully present and absorbed the moment?**

**How do you tend to live in extremes? Where in your life would you like to experience greater balance?**

**What will you do to cultivate the virtue of sobriety?**

> **→ Respond**
>
> The spiritual discipline of fasting will help you counter indulgent behavior. Practicing this discipline is as simple as giving up something you love (coffee, alcohol, social media, entertainment, etc.) and setting a timeline.

# Magic Carpet Ride

*"Be still, and know that I am God. I will be exalted among*

*the nations, I will be exalted in the earth!"*

—Psalm 46:10

IN THE 1992 CLASSIC DISNEY FILM, *ALADDIN,* the street-rat-turned-prince tells Jasmine, "We could get out of the palace, see the world … Do you trust me?"[2] Extending his hand, Aladdin invites the princess to join him on the iconic magic carpet ride. This unforgettable scene is the perfect metaphor for what it's like to be married to or friends with an Enthusiast: living with a Seven feels like being on a series of magical flights that constantly transport us from one place to another (oftentimes literally). So first, *thank you,* dear Seven, for helping us see "a whole new world."

> We need to find God, and He cannot be found in noise and restlessness. God is the friend of silence.
>
> —Mother Teresa[1]

One of your greatest strengths is your natural go-getter attitude. You are a mover and shaker;

---

1   Gordon MacDonald, *Ordering Your Private World* (Nashville, TN: Thomas Nelson, 2017), 129.

2   Aladdin, directed by Ron Clements and John Musker (Buena Vista Pictures, 1992).

someone who is going places. As a kid, you were likely told to slow down or maybe even disciplined—all for just being *you*. Don't ever let others shame you simply because they are jealous of or don't understand your joy. As Olympic runner Eric Liddell famously said, "I believe God made me for a purpose, but He also made me fast. And when I run, I feel His pleasure."[3] Run headlong into life's fullness, and feel God's delight as you do.

However, we must remember that our strengths, taken to an extreme, can become weaknesses. The growth work for every Seven is to learn how to master a healthier tempo of life. Unhealthy Sevens believe, *the faster the better, period.* They eat, talk, and think fast while cramming as many experiences as they can into each twenty-four-hour day.[4] But you will eventually drive off a cliff if you never take your foot off the gas—and sometimes (unintentionally of course), you will take loved ones with you. That's why it is so important to pay attention to the warning signals from those you trust. Though it may feel like they're driving too slow in the left lane, they will help prevent you from crashing and burning.

Refusing to down-shift into a lower gear may create conflict in your relationships that will inevitably lead to more pain later on. A friend of mine once said that being married to her Seven husband started off like a magic carpet ride but eventually felt like he'd grabbed her hand and tugged her through life without ever letting go. If an unhealthy Seven does not acknowledge the sense of chaos and exhaustion their loved ones may feel from being pulled in every direction and having to keep up, they may eventually be confronted with pent-up resentment or worse, abandonment. Have periodic "tempo checks" with your loved ones to see how they are handling your pace.

> You won't find emptiness but God's presence in stillness.

The lie Sevens believe is that they will die of pain and boredom if they slow down. But when healthy and embracing saner rhythms, most find they actually *love* their new pace of life. They discover that the structures and spiritual disciplines that

---

3  "Chariots of Fire." Chariots of Fire (1981) / Ian Charleson: Eric Liddell. Accessed June 26, 2023. https://www.imdb.com/title/tt0082158/characters/nm0153182.

4  Riso and Hudson, *Personality Types*, 276.

once felt limiting can accelerate growth, which brings just as much satisfaction as chasing something new or different.

***The Good News for Enthusiasts*** is you won't find emptiness but God's presence in stillness. As the psalmist writes, "Be still, and know that I am God."[5] Elijah learned this firsthand. After the showdown between the God of Israel and the prophets of Baal on Mount Carmel, the prophet fled into the wilderness, wanting to die after the spectacular revival he expected didn't come. While he hid in the craggy wilderness and wondered if God still cared about him and his needs, God sent an angel with food and water. Shortly after, at Mount Horeb, God famously spoke to Elijah—not in the fire, wind, or even the earthquake but in a gentle *whisper*.[6]

Today, let this story be a reminder that if you slow down enough to get away from the whirlwind of life and find solitude like Elijah did on Mount Horeb, you get to hear the gentle whisper of God speaking directly to your heart. Right now, quiet your racing mind, be still, and embrace silence—not as an enemy but as an invitation for God's voice to come and fill every void.

---

### → Pray

Father, thank You for creating me to be a fast mover who leads others to experience the Christian life as a thrilling adventure. Though I experience Your pleasure on the go, help me now to experience more of Your presence by slowing down. Remove my fear of silence and stillness, and reveal how those things can actually lead to greater joy.

---

5   Psalm 46:10

6   1 Kings 19:12

# Day 23 Reflections:

**Why would your loved ones be missing out if they didn't have you to get them out of "the palace" and show them the world?**

**What lies behind your drive to move through life at such a fast pace? What do you fear would happen if you slowed down?**

**Where in life do you need to pump the brakes? Give someone in your life the permission to tell you no or not right now.**

---

## ➜ Respond

Instead of jumping out of bed as soon as the alarm goes off or immediately grabbing your phone, spend a few minutes in silence, patiently listening for the gentle whisper of the Lord.

# Yoda Says: Be Present

*This is the day that the Lord has made; let us rejoice and be glad in it.*

—Psalm 118:24

IN THE OPENING TO *THE EMPIRE STRIKES Back*, the desperate Rebel Alliance is overpowered and almost annihilated by the Empire. After he escapes, our hero Luke Skywalker goes to the remote planet Dagobah to begin Jedi training with the great Master Yoda. But Luke's wanderlust for the future gets him reprimanded by his wise teacher, as Yoda tells him, "All his life has he looked away . . . to the future, to the horizon. Never his mind on where he was. Hmm? What he was doing. Hmph! Adventure. Heh! Excitement. Heh! A Jedi craves not these things. You are reckless!"[2] Similar to Luke, an Enthusiast may be tempted to dwell in the future, but to become one with the Force, one must live in the *present*.

> All his life has he looked away . . . to the future, to the horizon. Never his mind on where he was.
>
> –Yoda[1]

Enneagram author Sarajane Case, a Seven herself, shared that when she flew

1   "Star Wars: Episode V - the Empire Strikes Back," IMDb, accessed June 26, 2023, https://www.imdb.com/title/tt0080684/characters/nm0000568.

2   Ibid.

across the ocean and arrived at base of the iconic Eiffel Tower, the first thing she mentioned out loud to her friend was how excited she was about the road trip she was going to take when got back to the States! Case explains, "It's common for type sevens to find the most joy in preparation—the thoughts of their next big thing or their next exciting opportunity, and spending hours daydreaming, planning, and preparing for the next time they know they'll experience joy."[3] The big idea, according to Case, is this: "Living in the future is limiting the fullness you are experiencing in life."[4]

Sevens can experience more of that fullness by cultivating a sense of *wonder* for the present. Your childlike sense of awe for the future—the hereafter—can also be used as a strength to admire beauty in the *here and now*.[5] I heard a Type Four say they once pulled their car over on the side of the highway just to sit and absorb the stunning radiance of the morning sunrise. Take to heart the example of your Four brothers and sisters: find opportunities to stop and refocus your mind to experience fullness in the present before it vanishes. After all, the only thing we really ever have is the present—both the past and future are always only in our minds.

> Being present is an act of faith.

Being present is an *act of faith*. It's choosing to believe that because God loves you and will take care of your needs, He will not let you miss out on anything if you limit yourself to the present. Pastor A.J. Sherrill says that Sevens should set aside time every day for solitude and silence. He recommends carving out a sacred time right away in the morning, before the rush of the day, to look within and remember your identity is not based on how others feel about you but on God's pronouncement of belovedness over you.[6]

Similarly, Drew Moser suggests Sevens practice the ancient art of *Lectio Devina (or "Divine Readings")* as a way to be more present with God's Word. This contemplative practice approaches a small piece of Scripture as if it were a lavish

---

3   Case, *The Honest Enneagram*, 178.

4   Ibid., 178.

5   Carver and Green, *What's Your Enneatype?*, 130-131.

6   AJ Sherrill, *The Enneagram for Spiritual Formation: How Knowing Ourselves Can Make Us More Like Jesus* (Grand Rapids, MI: Brazos Press, a division of Baker Publishing Group, 2020), 77.

meal and requires you to slow down, read the passage carefully several times, and contemplate new insights that emerge with each pass.[7] Moser also recommends that future-oriented Sevens practice "Sacred Delay," which is slowing down to let your past catch up with you. By accessing past memories and feelings, you courageously engage your fear rather than running from it.[8]

***The Good News for Enthusiasts*** is that as good as tomorrow will be, we can rejoice in *today* for "this is the day that the LORD has made."[9] You can stop imagining what tomorrow will be like if you remember God is excited to be with you today: "in [God's] presence there is fullness of joy."[10] Just as Luke was charged with pulling his eyes away from the horizon and toward his present task—and, more importantly, just as Jesus got up early in the morning to find a solitary place to enjoy communion with His Father—so should you create a regular rhythm of solitude where you turn off the noise from all distractions. When you take that first step to draw near to the Lord, "he will rejoice over you with gladness; he will quiet you by his love; he will exult over you with loud singing."[11]

---

### → Pray

Father, thank You for being all-present. Remove the fear within that tries to convince me the present is dull, boring, or unfulfilling. Open up my spiritual eyes to see that You are with me right now, offering a feast if I'll slow down to enjoy it. Help me become more present with You and others by cultivating childlike wonder with the here and now.

---

7    Moser, *The Enneagram of Discernment*, 365.

8    Ibid., 362.

9    Psalm 118:24

10   Psalm 16:11

11   Zephaniah 3:17

# Day 24 Reflections:

**When have you caught yourself feeling unfulfilled just as you checked off one of your wish list or bucket list items?**

**What is beautiful about what you have or are experiencing in *this* present moment?**

**How will you implement the spiritual discipline of solitude in your life?**

---

### → Respond

Schedule a day of solitude in your calendar every four to six weeks to commune with God and answer the following questions: Where do I feel burdened? Where do I feel blessed? What do I feel God calling me to do? Where do I need to wait on God?

# Dinner Parties

*On this mountain the Lord of hosts will make for all peoples a*

*feast of rich food, a feast of well-aged wine, of rich food full of*

*marrow, of aged wine well refined. . . . He will swallow up death*

*forever; and the Lord God will wipe away tears from all faces.*

—Isaiah 25:6,8a

---

YOU MAY BE PLEASANTLY SURPRISED THAT MUCH of Jesus' ministry happened around a dinner table. Truly, the Gospels in general, and Luke's in particular, could be renamed *Meals with Jesus.*[2] My friend Chris says he's drawn to these passages because in them He experiences an earthy Jesus who offers grace, community, and mission around a dinner table.

> In approximately one-fifth of the sentences in Luke's Gospel and in Acts, meals play a conspicuous role.
>
> —Markus Barth[1]

---

1   Markus Barth, *Rediscovering the Lord's Supper: Communion with Israel, with Christ, and Among the Guests* (Eugene, OR: Wipf & Stock Publishers, 2006), 71.

2   Luke records Jesus' lunch with Levi (5:27-32), supper at Simon's (7:36-50), big picnic miracle (9:10-17), meal at Martha's (10:38-42), awkward conversations with the Pharisees (11:37-54; 14:1-11), "scandalous" meeting with Zacchaeus and those sinful tax collectors (19:1-10), Last Supper with his disciples (22:14-20), and breaking of bread on the road to Emmaus (24:13-35).

Our Savior wasn't afraid to go to parties that religious leaders would not dare attend. He was condemned by church people for showing hospitality to both righteous and sinners, rich and poor, Jew and Gentile: "The Son of Man came eating and drinking, and they say, 'Look at him! A glutton and a drunkard, a friend of tax collectors and sinners!' "[3] As a gatherer of people, your motives and actions will also be called into question, but take heart that the same Jesus in Luke's gospel is with you every time you open up your home. Around a table, you can put lost people's expectations about Jesus right side up, meeting their physical and spiritual needs as you prepare a feast of food and laughter, like the "agape meals" of the earliest Christ-followers. Jesus rolled like this: Dinner, *then* doctrine. As the popular saying goes, "No one cares how much you know until they know how much you care."[4]

Dinner parties also have the power to break down walls of hostility between ethnic lines. Unfortunately, Sunday morning is still one of the most segregated hours in American life. But you can change that. One of my favorite pastors, Bryan Loritts, says, "Sanctuaries reflect our dinner tables. So if you want a diverse sanctuary, then you have to have hundreds of diverse dinner tables."[5]

> The Father doesn't hold grudges, but throws grace parties.

Dinner tables are also the safest place for prodigals to return. In Day 9, we talked about how the Prodigal Son's "grass is greener" mentality caused him to squander away all of his father's inheritance like a bad trip to Vegas. Dirt poor, sitting among the pigs, he remembered his father and journeyed home, hoping at least for an honest way to earn his keep. Unexpectedly, the father had been waiting for his return and ran toward him, kissed and hugged him, covered up his rags with the best robe in the house, put shoes on his blistered feet, and slid the family ring on his hand.

Meanwhile, the older brother threw a pious tantrum. When the father hosted a welcome home dinner party, the older brother refused to go in. He couldn't

---

3   Matthew 11:19

4   This quote is often attributed to Theodore Roosevelt, but no known source can be found to verify.

5   "Building Bridges: An Interview with Bryan Loritts (Part 2)," Outreach Magazine, September 26, 2022, https://outreachmagazine.com/interviews/25967-bryan-loritts-building-bridges-part-2.html.

believe his irresponsible brother, who broke every rule in the family playbook, was getting off the hook. Religious types are allergic to grace, likely because they haven't experienced it themselves.

***The Good News for Enthusiasts*** is that the Father doesn't hold grudges, but throws grace parties. As you go about your day today, picture your heavenly Father waving His arms, inviting you to come in and eat with Him, no matter how wayward your past has been. If you've felt the overwhelming loving acceptance from being wrapped up in the arms of your gracious Father, use your gift of hospitality to invite the prodigals in your life to come into the party of grace. As you know, "there will be more joy in heaven over one sinner who repents than over ninety-nine righteous persons who need no repentance."[6]

Ultimately, your dinner table points others to the eternal party in heaven—where all dividing walls of hostility are broken down and abundance is the rule. The night before Jesus' life was taken, He promised His disciples, "I tell you I will not drink again of this fruit of the vine until that day when I drink it new with you in my Father's kingdom."[7] He was calling their attention to Isaiah's future vision of heaven's dinner table filled with the best foods and wine; a time when all God's promises are fulfilled for all of His wandering, scattered children. On that day, the fog machine and lights will come on, the vinyl turntables will start spinning, and our emcee will get up and shout, "Ain't no party like a Holy Ghost party 'cause a Holy Ghost party don't stop!"[8]

That's how this former deejay pictures it in my head anyway.

---

### → Pray

Father, the extravagant grace that You display in hosting parties for prodigals is utterly astonishing. Thank You for giving me the spiritual gift of hospitality, a much more powerful tool than knowledge to draw the lost back to Your loving arms. Though ninety-nine righteous people may not repent today, I will dance with You over the one sinner who does.

---

6   Luke 15:7

7   Matthew 26:29

8   "Holy Ghost Party (Live) - Forerunner Music & Cory Asbury," SongLyrics.com, accessed June 26, 2023, https://www.songlyrics.com/forerunner-music-cory-asbury/holy-ghost-party-live-lyrics/.

# Day 25 Reflections:

**Why does food and throwing parties make you unreasonably happy? What is inspiring about how Jesus ministered to people around meals?**

**Who can you invite over for dinner that doesn't look like you, belong to your political party, or embrace the same religious beliefs?**

**How will you use your gift of hospitality to host dinner parties at your house or plan socials for your church?**

---

## ➜ Respond

Build at least one meal into your small group rhythm each month. As you know, gathering around a dinner table builds a family-like community and creates a more welcoming environment for outsiders.

# Best-Friend Parenting

*My son, do not despise the Lord's discipline or be weary of his reproof, for the Lord reproves him whom he loves, as a father the son in whom he delights.*

—Proverbs 3:11-12

ENTHUSIASTS CAN MAKE INCREDIBLE PARENTS, CAREGIVERS, AND mentors. Prioritizing *connection* before *correction,* they are like big kids themselves, delightedly playing in the rain or making snow angels—even if their kids (or grandkids) aren't around! Enneagram author Jacqui Pollock explains that healthy Sevens bring the energy to their families, seeking out fun activities and exhilarating adventures, adding richness through your imagination and storytelling. You find opportunities to help children discover the magical world around them and encourage exploration and risk-taking. You use your quick thinking to help children find solutions to their problems and use your enduring optimism to help your family overcome challenges and keep moving forward.[1]

> All freedom comes from discipline.
>
> –Aristotle

---

1    Tressider, Loftus, and Pollock, *Knowing Me, Knowing Them,* 128-129.

But there is always a shadow. Pollock goes on to explain the negative effects of an unhealthy Seven: When your energy is unbridled, it may overwhelm your family and leave them feeling unheard. When you overcommit to new things, it may force you to sacrifice quality time with your family. After all, if you are always running late or can't follow through on promises, you may be seen as unreliable, impulsive, or immature. Due to your egalitarian approach to authority, you also may have unclear boundaries between parent and child.[2]

But all is not lost! Let's look at some strategies for growing as a parent, caregiver, or mentor. First, practice saying no to new ideas and opportunities and bring family projects to a close before starting new ones. Respect your children's differences—especially the ones who are more structured, shy, or melancholy. Knowing your proclivity to positivity, don't try to cheer your family up all the time; some things can only be learned through hardship. Also, allow your children to go at their own pace instead of yours, and intentionally create more space to deeply listen and make them feel heard and understood.[3]

> If you don't lovingly discipline others, you're limiting their potential rather than leading them to freedom.

Minimize relational conflict by paying attention to your unique stress triggers, which often include feeling unjustly criticized, running out of time to do all the fun things you wanted, or feeling limited or suffocated by the responsibilities of caring for others. When your children are negative, pessimistic, melancholy, or turn down new opportunities or social functions, you can feel triggered by "sympathetic FOMO."[4] If you can catch yourself when feeling these things, it'll help you take responsibility for them and prevent you from becoming critical toward those you love.

One of those passages a Seven would prefer to skip over is the latter part of Hebrews 12. Sure, the beginning of the chapter is great: the author admonishes the saints to run the race of faith well. That's inspiring. But this calling *also*

---

2   Ibid., 130-131.

3   Ibid., 135-138.

4   Ibid., 131-133.

includes enduring hostility from our enemies as well as discipline from the Lord. Not as inspiring at first glance! The author, taking his cue from the Proverbs, says, "For the Lord disciplines the one he loves, and chastises every son whom he receives. … For the moment all discipline seems painful rather than pleasant, but later it yields the peaceful fruit of righteousness to those who have been trained by it."[5]

Remember, if you don't lovingly discipline others, you're limiting their potential rather than leading them to freedom. "Best-friend parenting" provides children with way too many gifts and soft (or absent) structure, which ultimately ends up harming them—keeping them from being effective parents when they grow up. So make sure to be friendly to your children without trying to be their best friend.

***The Good News for Enthusiasts*** is that if you as a child of God can get through the unpleasant part of discipline, allowing the Father to tell you no, limit you, or hold you accountable to the rules, then you will experience the long-lasting peace that comes from renewed character, conscience, and conduct. Then and only then will you be able to help the young ones under your care experience that same kind of peace.

### → Pray

Father, thank You for giving me energy, an imaginative mind, and childlike joy to enrich the lives of those under my care. I love the way I'm wired. Now, help me see the significance of discipline although it feels very unpleasant. I will receive Your loving correction today, knowing You are leading me out of bondage to sin into greater peace and freedom.

---

5  Hebrews 12:6,11

# Day 26 Reflections:

How have your unique strengths positively impacted the children in your life?

How have you seen any unhealthy tendencies or stress triggers negatively affect the children in your life?

What opportunities are there in your home, extended family, or church community to teach and model the gospel for children or teens?

→ **Respond**

If you are a parent, schedule a weekly fun "date" with each of your children, and let them pick the place and activity. If you aren't a parent, look for an opportunity to come alongside a family this week and offer your support!

*Day 27:*

# The Miraculous Lunch Box

*But Jesus said, "They need not go away; you give them something*

*to eat." They said to him, "We have only five loaves here and*

*two fish." And he said, "Bring them here to me."*

—Matthew 14:16-18

---

HAVE YOU EVER BEEN "HANGRY?" WHEN YOU haven't eaten in a while, the level of sugar in your blood decreases, which activates cortisol (the stress hormone) and adrenaline (your fight-or-flight hormone). This can interfere with higher brain functions, causing you to lose impulse control and become short-tempered.[2] Hunger turns into anger quickly, and even the nicest adults (and all children!) start to get really irritated. Though you've convinced yourself zombies aren't real, you start to act like one—an unthinking creature of pure craving.

> As God is my witness, I will never go hungry again!
>
> –Scarlett O'Hara, *Gone With The Wind*[1]

Jesus and His disciples were close to experiencing a zombie apocalypse when they were surrounded by over

---

1   "Gone with the Wind," IMDb, accessed June 27, 2023, https://www.imdb.com/title/tt0031381/characters/nm0000046.

2   "Is Being 'Hangry' Really a Thing or Just an Excuse?," Cleveland Clinic, June 7, 2021, https://health.clevelandclinic.org/is-being-hangry-really-a-thing-or-just-an-excuse/.

five thousand increasingly hangry people in the Judean countryside. (This was obviously before Jesus-followers mastered the art of pre-ordering Chick-Fil-A for large groups.) So the disciples came to Jesus and recommended that everyone find a nearby town and get some food, a more difficult plan in those days than it sounds, which may be why Jesus had a different idea. He told the disciples: "You give them something to eat."[3] First of all, this request would have been annoying to the average Enthusiast because they've learned to live independently and believe in their inherent self-sufficiency. Some of the disciples may have been thinking, *Those needy people aren't my responsibility! Their lack of planning is not my emergency.*

The second reason Jesus' command would've been hard to hear is due to Sevens' fear of *deprivation.* Their collected savings wouldn't be enough to offer each person a bite, much less a meal. The lie Sevens tend to believe is: "I'm on my own. No one is going to take care of me or support me. It's up to me to fulfill my needs." In this brief moment, I'm sure the disciples felt like Jesus was not only out of touch with reality (or hangry himself!) but mistaken regarding who was responsible for whom.

> Abundance most often hides beneath a few broken pieces.

But the God who created our abundant world *ex nihilo* (literally "out of nothing")[4] was ready to give them yet another sign that the Divine was among them. After Andrew pointed out a boy who had five loaves and two fish, Jesus took the boy's lunch box and miraculously multiplied it to exponential proportions—so much that every person on that hillside ate their fill, and they had twelve baskets of leftovers![5]

The lesson in this incredible story is that abundance most often hides beneath a few broken pieces—a fact that goes beyond our physical sustenance and encapsulates our very lives. Just as the disciples could feed the large crowd with some scraps, so too can you feed the needy among you today. Don't be overwhelmed with

---

3   Matthew 14:16

4   Nicholas Bunnin and Jijuan Yu, *The Blackwell Dictionary of Western Philosophy* (Hoboken, NJ: Wiley-Blackwell, 2009), 149.

5   John 6:9-13

others' needs—God's not expecting you to give more than you have but to see that this world holds more than appearances would suggest. A simple word of encouragement, a small gift, or a few minutes of your time—in Christ's hands—can be blessed, broken, and turned into a spiritual meal for others.

***The Good News for Enthusiasts*** is that you will be taken care of. *We all* will be taken care of. We don't worship the God of scarcity but of abundance! Our "original sin" is *taking* what would have been offered freely in due time. God is not stingy with the blessings of the world, but as the psalmist proclaimed, "He satisfies the longing soul, and the hungry soul he fills with good things."[6] Near the end of Jesus' earthly ministry, on the night He was betrayed, "He took bread, and after blessing it broke it and gave it to [His disciples], and said, 'Take; this is my body.'"[7] We remember these words every time we receive communion with the saints, reminding ourselves to open our hands to the One whose resources are ever-new.

> **→ Pray**
>
> Father, thank You for sending Your Son Jesus to become poor so that I might become rich.[8] Help me look at the scraps in my lunch box and see amazing potential. Remind me that the little I have is more than enough for others to feast on God's love. Today, I commit to letting You bless me, break me, and give me away so that I can welcome the needy with Jesus' compassion rather than send them away.

---

6 Psalm 107:9

7 Mark 14:22

8 2 Corinthians 8:9

# Day 27 Reflections:

**Where does the fear of being deprived show up in your life? In other words, how do you typically go about getting your needs met?**

**What memories from your past may be reinforcing the lie that you are on your own and that God (or others) won't take care of or support you?**

**In what ways does Jesus' miracle alter your outlook on the extent of what God can achieve through you when you feel empty-handed like the disciples?**

---

### ➺ Respond

Because Sevens rarely let others know when they need help but desperately long to be supported, step out of your comfort zone and share your sadness, hurts, or needs with someone so that they have an opportunity to take care of you.

# The Missing Piece

*Truly, I say to you, whoever does not receive the*

*kingdom of God like a child shall not enter it.*

—Mark 10:15

"It was missing a piece. And it was not happy."

These are the first words of author Shel Silverstein's charming fable about a circular creature that is missing a piece of itself. So sure it was meant to be complete, it sets out, singing:

> It is a Christian duty, as you know, for everyone to be as happy as he can.
>
> —C.S. Lewis[1]

Oh, I'm lookin' for my missin' piece
I'm lookin' for my missin' piece
Hi-dee-ho, here I go
Lookin' for my missin' piece.[2]

On this dangerous quest to complete itself—falling into holes and bumping into walls, testing

---

1  Wayne Martindale and Jerry Root, *The Quotable Lewis* (Carol Stream, IL: Tyndale House Publishers, 2012), 68.

2  "The Missing Piece," The Prindle Institute for Ethics, accessed June 12, 2023, https://www.prindleinstitute.org/books/the-missing-piece/.

and trying many different potential matches—the almost-circle finally finds the perfect wedge. But with the circle complete, it no longer has a mouth to sing and finds itself rolling much too fast to talk to a worm or smell a butterfly. Its belief of completion leaves it unable to travel slow enough to receive life as it comes. So, it puts down the missing piece and decides to keep searching.

The Enthusiast is also on a never-ending search for their life's missing piece. Similar to the Type Four, they firmly believe *something somewhere* can fill the aching void in their heart. They are always on the hunt for the never-ending high: maybe it's an interesting person, fun adventure, new travel destination, promising business pursuit, or sampling the finest foods and best wines. I've heard it said that Sevens have champagne running through their veins—they are the hedonists (a word that gets far too bad a reputation!) among us who believe the main purpose in this life is to *enjoy* it. They have a "fun filter" that tells them if something is not fun, it's not worth doing. However, Sevens often feel let down when their dream finally comes true and it doesn't live up to their expectations.[3]

On the positive side, you as a Seven teach us pursuing pleasure is good—and even the search and waiting themselves have value. As the famous artist Andy Warhol said, "The idea of waiting for something makes it more exciting."[4] You are like a care-free child playing in the sandbox, exploring God's breathtaking world in a way it was meant to be enjoyed. After all, Jesus once declared: "Truly, I say to you, whoever does not receive the kingdom of God like a child shall not enter it."[5] In healthy situations, children receive their gifts with natural gratitude and have no thought of earning them; they feel no guilt from life's gifts. Why should they? They simply receive the Father's gifts with open hands and enjoy them.

Now comes the "but" part. If you've been around any child for long, you know they can overdo it when it comes to pleasure. They relentlessly pursue their

---

3    Cron and Stabile, *The Road Back to You*, 216.

4    C Sreechinth, *Painted Words of Andy Warhol: 300+ Andy Warhol Quotes* (Scotts Valley, CA: CreateSpace Independent Publishing Platform, 2018), 37.

5    Mark 10:15

desires and avoid pain and boredom at all costs. They may plead with you to allow them to bend the rules and convince you they have enough self-control to not get addicted to social media, video games, and sugar. But as you know, they are deceived.

Left unchecked, in adulthood, Helen Palmer says that unhealthy Sevens may become "soft narcissists." Although they may not look like "my way or the highway" kinds of prideful leaders, they still choose a path where they can get their way, rationalize (or spiritualize) their selfish course of action, and then minimize the consequences of their decisions.[6]

***The Good News for Enthusiasts*** is you don't have to try and fill the void within through tirelessly pursuing that "missing piece." Any piece you do find, though it may seem to fit perfectly for a while, will inevitably leave you incomplete. As actor Jim Carrey said, "I think everybody should get rich and famous and do everything they ever dreamed of so they can see that it's not the answer."[7]

Thankfully, God has offered Himself as our missing piece. He invites us to live *from His* pleasure rather than *for our* pleasure. When you operate from God's pleasure, which is selfless in nature, you will widen your perspective to include the good of others as you pursue God's gifts with anticipation. Continue to explore the world with childlike wonder, but never lose sight of the One whose completeness fills every part of you.

---

### → Pray

Father, You are my missing piece. Forgive me for running after worldly pleasures and hurting people along the way. As I go about my day, I ask that Your Spirit would free me from selfishness so that I can pursue Your pleasures with the good of others in mind.

---

6　Palmer, *The Enneagram in Love and Work*, 182.

7　"A Thought." The Knoxville News-Sentinel, June 22, 2007, Quote Page B4, Column 3, Knoxville, Tennessee. (Newspapers.com).

# Day 28 Reflections:

**How have you noticed an ability to enjoy God's creation in a way that others find challenging?**

**What is something that you waited for with great anticipation, but it didn't live up to your expectations? What did you learn from that experience?**

**What will you do to acknowledge the feelings and feedback of others the next time you have an exciting idea?**

## ➜ Respond

Identify one trigger that leads to impulsive behavior and work to avoid it. For example, if you overspend when shopping online, delete your shopping app or limit your access to credit cards.

# Escape Artist

*Then Jesus was led up by the Spirit into the*

*wilderness to be tempted by the devil.*

—Matthew 4:1

---

E.B. WHITE, AUTHOR OF THE CHILDREN'S BOOK *Charlotte's Web*, in Seven-like fashion humorously said, "I get up every morning determined to both change the world and have one hell of a good time. Sometimes this makes planning my day difficult."[2] Yet Enthusiasts are actually master planners: "It's thrilling to think of possibilities," one Seven explained, "and I don't mind navigating the red tape to make things happen. When a new idea comes to me, I sit up straight, my body twitches, and I am filled with endorphins. There's nothing quite like the joy of planning and pulling off something that is tons of fun and makes people happy."[3]

> The two enemies of human happiness are pain and boredom.
>
> –Arthur Schopenhauer[1]

---

1   Arthur Schopenhauer, *The Wisdom of Life And Other Essays* (New York, NY: M. Walter Dunne, 1901), 18.

2   Guy Kawasaki, *Reality Check: The Irreverent Guide to Outsmarting, Outmanaging, and Outmarketing Your Competition* (New York, NY: Portfolio, Published by the Penguin Group, 2008), 71.

3   Vancil, *Self to Lose Self to Find*, 113.

Don't ever take this ability for granted. Use it to help those around you find solutions to complex problems, generate new ideas, or discover new opportunities; remember, this comes more naturally for you than others. However, you must also know you can use your superpower to become an escape artist.

In the early scenes of Disney and Pixar's *Up* (previously mentioned on Day 17), we see young Carl holding a balloon with the phrase "The Spirit of Adventure" scribbled on it, a heavily-symbolic balloon perfectly illustrates the spirit of wonderment that every Seven carries with them. But after Carl suffers the tragic loss of his wife and becomes an embittered and lonely elderly man, the local authorities come to send him off to a retirement facility. To escape this fate, Carl ties hundreds of helium-filled balloons to his home and floats "up" and out of the city and on to adventure.[4]

In similar fashion, unhealthy Sevens can use their superpower of planning to make a beeline toward the clouds and escape from reality. They actively tie together a bundle of fun and stimulating experiences to float above all the boredom, limitations, sadness, discomfort, or pain of life.[5] Sevens are "escapologists" who are always planning ahead and looking for an escape hatch in case they get caught in a boring conversation, unpleasant interaction, or uncomfortable relationship.[6] They are master magicians, pulling off a disappearing act better than anyone.

> All great stories include both pain and pleasure.

But if you learn to face your fears and not run to your drug of choice—whether it be the "classics" like drinking, gambling, partying, and sex or the less noticed drugs like new relationships, jobs, or travel—you will find that the truth is not so scary after all. Working through your fears will give you more endurance to be present with others when your head is trying to find the exit sign. To experience more fulfilling relationships, a Seven must learn how to be silent, rest, and just sit with others, especially in unpleasant circumstances. You must allow yourself to

---

4   Alexandra @ The Dream of Pixar, "'Up' Themes: Relationships," The Dream of Pixar, March 15, 2011, https://thedreamofpixar.wordpress.com/2011/03/14/up-themes-relationships/.

5   Chestnut, *The Complete Enneagram*.

6   Cron and Stabile, *The Road Back to You*, 215.

go through a dark night of the soul, digesting your regrets and painful memories to fully mature into the kind of human your family and friends need.

Jesus went through a dark night of the soul right after His baptism, when the true Spirit of Adventure, who would take Jesus into the clouds at the end of His earthly ministry, took Him into the desert at the start of His ministry. He was deprived of food for forty days and forty nights while being tempted by the devil.[7] If He came for Jesus, then be prepared for the Spirit to lead you into the desert of your inner life so that He can prepare your character for your calling.[8]

***The Good News for Enthusiasts*** is that while Jesus was in the wilderness, "the devil left him, and behold, angels came and were ministering to him."[9] God will also be with you in your dark night of the soul: there's nothing to fear. Today, try to catch yourself when your attention moves too quickly toward the future. The worldview of a Seven is this: without God, I see the world as limited and must race to plan new ideas and paths, but *with* God, I can stop to receive His joy now in the present. Remember, all great stories include both pain and pleasure: Do you want a boring story? Then avoid pain. But if you want a great one, then learn to live in the dark as well as the light.

---

### → Pray

Father, give me the clarity to discern between healthy pursuits and escapism. Forgive me for seeking refuge from my fears instead of facing them head-on. I know You have not given me a spirit of fear but of power and love.[10] Don't allow fear to paralyze me when I'm in the dark, holding me back from my true potential.

---

7   Matthew 4:1-11

8   Sherrill, *The Enneagram for Spiritual Formation*, 77.

9   Matthew 4:11

10   2 Timothy 1:7

# Day 29 Reflections:

When have you allowed yourself to feel negative emotions without running away from them? How did this show growth and maturity? Give yourself credit for facing these emotions head-on.

Where in your life right now are you seeking an escape, hoping to avoid some uncomfortable relationship or commitment?

How does your constant planning hinder your ability to be present with your pain, fear, or sadness? Can you identify any cues or triggers that can help you relax your urge to escape?

---

## → Respond

Set aside a specific time each week to start journaling to help you become more aware of your emotions, which can help you identify the underlying causes of your escapism.

# Delayed Gratification

*And let us not grow weary of doing good, for in due*

*season we will reap, if we do not give up.*

—Galatians 6:9

AT THE YOUNG AGE OF TWENTY-FOUR, MY friend Austin was invited to start a new church in a college town. Despite envisioning the impact he could have, the reality was far from glamorous. He faced financial struggles, disappointment, criticism, and even tasks like cleaning toilets. A few years later Austin shared a heartfelt message to a room full of pastors called, "What did we sign up for?" where he made the vulnerable admission to us that, had he known what it would entail, he might have said no to this invitation.

Be careful not to compromise what you want most for what you want now.

-Zig Ziglar[1]

Austin's story first and foremost is a good reminder to take Jesus' lesson on counting the cost[2] very seriously because average Sevens don't often finish what they start. You can protect yourself and prevent a lot of

---

1   Donna R Ryan, *Equipped to Tell the Next Generation* (Eugene, OR: Wipf & Stock Publishers, 2020), 73.

2   Luke 14:28-30

heartache if you do a full risk analysis when planning your next big idea: look *before* you leap so that you don't take a hard fall. That said, as Austin shared, it's often a good thing we don't know how tough things can get, otherwise we might never leap at all.

One of the great things about Sevens is their spontaneity. When I was hosting an Enneagram conference for a church in Iowa, one of the Sevens participating in our panel discussion felt the room needed an energy boost, so he stood up and ran around the room, forcing the crowd to do the wave with him. Antics like that are why we love Sevens so much! But there is a difference between *spontaneity* and *impulsivity*.

Because average Sevens crave satisfaction through stimulation, they will often respond impulsively to distractions without delay. The good news (for me, at least) is that my Seven friends always text me back right away— anything to follow the next distraction! But this same impulsivity can result in major problems for the Seven, including over-eating, drinking, or pushing yourself too hard and stretching yourself too thin. Riso and Hudson share that impulsivity can also lead you to develop ideas or projects that are only half-baked, which can cause others to see you as impatient or superficial. Though Sevens are often smart and talented, you may become an "instant expert" on many topics or skills without mastering any of them thoroughly.[3]

> Impulsivity can also lead you to develop ideas or projects that are only half-baked.

Author Saranjane Case reminds her fellow Sevens, "All ideas aren't for you to create. You are not responsible for bringing to life every single idea that comes to your mind. You aren't missing out on anything if you put that idea in a safe place and let it stay there for a while. … I just recommend writing them down somewhere safe, and when the time is right, you can revisit the list. Give your projects time to be successful, or you will struggle for the rest of your life."[4]

---

3   Riso and Hudson, *The Wisdom of the Enneagram*, 280-281.

4   Case, *The Honest Enneagram*, 177.

In today's fast-paced world, we want things quickly, whether it is fast food, fast internet, or fast results. But sometimes, delayed gratification can be a blessing in disguise. Today's verse from Galatians reminds us to keep doing what is right, even if it won't "feel good" till later.

By the way, Austin is now thirty-one years old and still faithfully leading his flock. Because he didn't give up when things got tough, he was able to see an inner-city high school ministry launched, thousands of college students reached, and hundreds of people baptized in his church—including his mother! Austin said God did incredibly more than he signed up for.

***The Good News for Enthusiasts*** is if you resist the temptation of an instant reward, you'll reap a greater reward later. Jesus showed us the value of delayed gratification by enduring pain, suffering, and humiliation on the cross. He never gave up. In the same way, make a decision now to stay in the same church, same friend group, same job, or same path for the next few years even when these cease to be fun, easy, or interesting. You will be surprised by the stories you'll be able to share at the end of the road.

---

## → Pray

Father, I'm thankful Your Son, Jesus, did not quit when things got tough but endured to the end. Help me to have patience and perseverance as I continue to do good, even when I do not see immediate results. By the power of the Holy Spirit, produce in me the fruit of self-control so that I can overcome the allure of instant rewards in exchange for eternal ones.

# Day 30 Reflections:

When have you intentionally practiced delayed gratification and experienced the rewards of patience and self-control? How did that experience shape your character and draw you closer to God?

Do a time audit of the past seven days. How much of your time did you spend seeking instant rewards versus cultivating long-term projects or relationships?

What meaningful commitments do you want to keep? What will you do to prevent yourself from jumping on and riding the next fun wave that appears?

## → Respond

Practice delayed gratification by setting a block of time during the day or prolonged waiting period for habits such as eating, shopping purchases, and social media.

# Don't Skip This One

*It is better to go to the house of mourning than to go to the house of feasting.*

—Ecclesiastes 7:2a

"JESUS WEPT."[1] THOSE WORDS REPEATED THROUGH MY lowered head as I sat at my desk, my own tears welling up. A long road of infertility had rocked my marriage, leaving crushed dreams and hopes deferred. Experiences like this are difficult for anyone, but when the ones from whom you seek comfort grieve differently, it can add alienation and loneliness to the pain.

For years, my wife, Lindsey, wept, believing we'd never see the miracle we longed for—and to this day, still no miracle. I didn't cry but kept telling her to "have faith." Looking back, I can see now that what I had was not faith but naivety. (Sidenote: I have also come to see how hurtful it is to tell anyone who's struggling to simply "have faith"; trite answers are never helpful, even if they are from Scripture.) While

> When someone's telling you a sad story and crying, how long should I wait before I take a bite of my corn dog?
>
> —Anonymous

1   John 11:35

she cried, I suppressed my emotions by naively assuming everything would work out, but this was just an unconscious strategy to sweep things under the rug. In so doing, I suppressed Lindsey's pain, dodged her emotions, failed to offer the living presence of the Christ, and held fast to stoicism when I should have been sowing tears.

Thankfully, we joined a small group of believers who felt stuck in various ways. During one of our sessions, the leader pointed his finger at me and sternly said, "David was a man who grieved and was called a man after God's own heart. You haven't done that." Those stern words shocked me out of passivity, and the next morning, as I sat reading the story of Lazarus, I finally broke open. Coming across the powerfully short line, "Jesus wept," I heard God tell me: "Lindsey's tears are My tears." And for the first time since we began our struggle, I wept too.

Embracing God's invitation to weep feels very counterintuitive. You may say to yourself, "Life can be hard, but why wallow in it?" "Why not look on the bright side?" or "With a little faith, everyone should be able to stay positive regardless of the circumstances." This is because Sevens can quickly acknowledge positive emotions like happiness and excitement but find it much more difficult to find validity in life's darker corners.

> Help us walk courageously through the pain rather than find the quickest way around it.

While Sevens' humor and ability to mine silver linings in even the darkest valleys is a true gift, they can also use it as a shortcut to skip over empathy and grief. At funerals, they may proclaim how incredible it is that their loved one is in paradise while others are still tearfully contemplating their relational loss. My friend and Enthusiast Amy Wicks puts the problem this way: "Sevens can try to rip the grave clothes off too quickly."

One helpful passage for all Sevens is Ecclesiastes 7:2, in which the Teacher reminds us, "It is better to go to the house of mourning than to go to the house of feasting." Earlier in chapter three, the Wise Sage explains that we should create space for both weeping and laughing, mourning and dancing.[2] The point is: God has ordained that we party hard and enjoy lots of recreation but also that we set aside hours, days, or perhaps a *season* to mourn tragedy or death. He wants us to contemplate the brevity and fragility of human life, reflecting on our mortality and prioritizing an eternal perspective.

***The Good News for Enthusiasts*** is "The Lord is near to the brokenhearted and saves the crushed in spirit."[3] Underline the word "near" in that verse. When your heart gets broken or you are crushed with anxiety, the Lord draws *near* to you. He will not often provide answers, but He will always show up, drawing near with His quiet presence and empathetic tears to sit in the perplexity of darkness and loss, rather than swoop in to offer artificial cheer or false reassurances. This is what Jesus' incarnation was all about and is at the heart of His command to "go and do likewise"[4]: you are called to become the friend we need during loss or heartache. Help us walk courageously through the pain rather than find the quickest way around it.

---

### → Pray

Father, give me the courage to grieve and lament, knowing it is a necessary part of healing and growth. Help me navigate the depths of my emotions, offering them to You with brutal honesty and vulnerability. Finally, give me strength to draw near to others in their time of grief rather than distancing myself or offering emotional shortcuts.

---

2   Ecclesiastes 3:4; We have much to learn from our Jewish brothers and sisters, who build periods of mourning into their lives, such as the practice of "sitting shiva" when someone in your community experiences loss.

3   Psalm 34:18

4   Luke 10:37

# Day 31 Reflections:

**Have you ever found it difficult to grieve or empathize with someone else's pain? How did you handle that situation, and what did you learn from it?**

**Why are you tempted to rush through the grieving process and "rip the grave clothes off too quickly?" How does Ecclesiastes affirm the value and benefit of sadness and lament?**

**What can you do to hold space with others who are experiencing loss or heartache?**

---

### ➜ Respond

Think about a painful experience and then write a prayer of lament using Psalm 22 as a guide. Express your grief over the loss of a loved one, personal failure or disappointments, unfulfilled dreams, childhood experiences, or social injustice.

# The Gift of ADHD

*For you formed my inward parts; you knitted me together in my*

*mother's womb. I praise you, for I am fearfully and wonderfully*

*made. Wonderful are your works; my soul knows it very well.*

—Psalm 139:13-14

---

LET'S GET ONE THING CLEAR AT THE outset: not all Enneagram Sevens have ADHD, and not all individuals with ADHD are Sevens. However, it's common for Enthusiasts to exhibit ADHD characteristics, which can present challenges in attention, focus, impulsivity, memory, time management, and social-emotional aspects. My friend Chris experienced a shift in expectations as he entered midlife, leading to guilt and shame as he wondered why he couldn't conform to speaking slower, increased structure, longer meetings, or lower energy levels like other leaders.

> I may have ADHD, but God's grace is my superpower.
>
> –Jonathan Mooney

In an article for *The Guardian*, Noelle Faulkner shared her journey of burnouts and misdiagnosis until her thirties, shedding light on the lack of understanding and research on ADHD in women. Faulkner highlighted ADHD association with disruptive behavior in boys, but for girls, it can instead foster feelings of never being good enough.[1] Women with ADHD, whom Faulkner referred to as the "lost girls," often mask their symptoms and face perfectionism, low self-esteem, and inadequacy.

Man or woman, these struggles may make you question your ability to fully embrace God's purpose for your life, but never forget how God fearfully and wonderfully made you, knitting you together in your mother's womb. As my friend Elvin puts it, your unique wiring as a Seven doesn't make you deficient but *different*. Mozart showed signs of ADHD from childhood. Reviewers in the *Journal of Neurology, Neurosurgery, and Psychiatry* concluded that his exceptional creativity stemmed not only from his abilities but also his distinctive cognitive and neurological function.[2]

Mozart's life serves as an example of turning apparent disadvantages into advantages. Sevens with ADHD traits exhibit remarkable creativity and lateral thinking, making unique connections, and generating original ideas. Bouts of hyperfocus can be leveraged to yield the results of years in days, and their high energy and enthusiasm bring excitement and passion to projects while spontaneity and flexibility foster adaptability and exploration in others as well.

> Your ADHD is not a limitation but an invitation for God's power to be perfected in your life.

Every natural gift comes with challenges. To overcome some of these challenges, consider implementing the following strategies: Establish routines and structures in your daily life to create organization and predictability. Break down big tasks into smaller steps, celebrating each achievement along the way. Set clear goals and prioritize what matters most to you. When working, find a quiet space or use headphones to minimize distractions. Use colorful labels, sticky notes, or visual reminders to enhance memory. Time management techniques, like

---

1   Noelle Faulkner, "The Lost Girls: 'Chaotic and Curious, Women with ADHD All Have Missed Red Flags That Haunt Us," The Guardian, November 1, 2020, https://www.theguardian.com/society/2020/nov/02/the-lost-girls-chaotic-and-curious-women-with-adhd-all-have-missed-red-flags-that-haunt-us.

2   Aidin Ashoori and Joseph Jankovic, "Mozart's Movements and Behaviour: A Case of Tourette's Syndrome?," Journal of neurology, neurosurgery, and psychiatry, November 2007, https://www.ncbi.nlm.nih.gov/pmc/articles/PMC2117611/

time blocking, can be helpful for making the most of your day. If needed, don't hesitate to request accommodations from your employer, such as flexible work hours or modified environments. Take care of yourself through exercise, proper nutrition, sufficient sleep, and stress management. With the right strategies and support, individuals with ADHD—or its characteristics—can thrive personally and professionally.

***The Good News for Enthusiasts*** is you don't have to be afraid to openly talk about your mental health struggle. Your ADHD is not a limitation but an invitation for God's power to be perfected in your weakness. Remember, you are not defined by ADHD or any other diagnosis: You are a beloved child of God, chosen and cherished. Be kind and patient with yourself, celebrating even the smallest progress. He is continually shaping you into the person He created you to be. Keep seeking Him, leaning on His promises, and trusting in His unwavering love. You've got this!

---

### → Pray

Father, I confess it can be challenging and discouraging at times to navigate the modern world as a Seven, but I know Your grace is sufficient for me. Help me embrace my weaknesses and trust in Your strength. Guide me and equip me for every task and responsibility. Use my journey with ADHD to bring glory to Your name and to bless others.

---

# Day 32 Reflections:

**How can you embrace and celebrate your unique wiring as a Seven, including any ADHD traits you may have, knowing God fearfully and wonderfully made you?**

**In what ways can you turn what may seem like disadvantages into advantages, leveraging your creativity, hyperfocus, resilience, and other strengths for the glory of God?**

**Which one of the proactive strategies listed above can you try right away to help overcome your challenges?**

---

### ➜ Respond

Despite any reservations you may have, seeking professional guidance and considering medication has proven beneficial for many Sevens with ADHD, helping them cope effectively in various aspects of life. Consider consulting your doctor if today's reading resonated with you.

# The Discipline of Celebration

*When Miriam the prophetess, the sister of Aaron, took a tambourine in her hand, and all the women went out after her with tambourines and dancing.*

—Exodus 15:20

LET'S TALK ABOUT SOMETHING YOU'RE NATURALLY GREAT at: celebration! Celebration serves multiple purposes and brings so much joy, connecting people, strengthening bonds, and creating a sense of accomplishment and boosting morale for individuals and teams. Celebrations honor traditions, preserve heritage, and foster a sense of identity.

> The decision to set the mind on the higher things of life is an act of the will. That is why celebration is a discipline.
>
> —Richard Foster[1]

But why aren't we always good at celebrating? Well, some of us focus too much on future goals or urgent tasks while others think everything must be perfect before celebrating. I get it—even I haven't thrown a launch party for the book series I've published—and this is the seventh book! Sometimes we think it's vain to celebrate ourselves, but those reasons don't hold up, do they?

---

1   Richard Foster, "The Art of Celebration," Boundless, November 30, 1BC, https://www.boundless.org/faith/the-art-of-celebration/.

When the discipline of celebration is neglected, we don't stop to acknowledge the work of the Spirit and immediately move on to the next challenge. In doing so, we train ourselves to believe what we've accomplished or experienced isn't important or worthwhile, resulting in a cycle of feeling like we are never enough.

But you, dear Enthusiast, are the break in the clouds. Celebration comes naturally to you. You're fantastic at spotting what God is doing in and around you.

In Scripture, celebration was both spontaneous and planned. After God saved His children from the hand of Pharaoh and they traveled miraculously through the Red Sea, Miriam the prophetess picked up a tambourine and led the women in an impromptu dance and song. Later, to celebrate the rededication of Jerusalem's walls, the Israelites recruited two choirs and rounded up the best musicians for a big party. Celebration and the remembrance of salvation past and ongoing was even written into their calendar! Ancient Israel gathered three times every year to celebrate God and His mighty acts through festival holidays. Likewise, the traditional church has followed Israel's lead, with a calendar marking seasons and days of expectancy, celebration, and confession.[2]

> Cultivating an attitude of gratitude takes intentionality.

So, how will you plan to celebrate? How will you create space for joys past and present? Remember, cultivating an attitude of gratitude takes *intentionality and openness to recognizing success.*

***The Good News for Enthusiasts*** is that the Spirit is always working. The question for you is, *Are you celebrating the work?* To become more intentional with your spiritual gift of celebration, begin your conversations and team meetings with the question: *Where have we seen God working?* Create space to acknowledge and appreciate achievements, milestones, and successes—no matter how small they seem. Mark special occasions on the calendar, like birthdays, holidays, or other important dates and create celebrations around them. Establish yearly customs, traditions, or excursions that symbolize and mark moments of celebration. These

---

2   Examples: Advent is about expectancy for Christ's appearing; Christmas is the celebration of his arrival and revealing; Lent and Holy Week are the desert of testing and sharing in his passion; Easter is joy at his defeat of death with everlasting life; and Pentecost is celebrating the Holy Spirit's descent onto all creation.

could involve storytelling, memorable meals, or repeat activities that bring joy and connection.

I know many of these practical suggestions seem obvious and you are already doing some of them, but discipline yourself to answer the reflection questions on the next page. With a little more intentionality and organization, you can leverage your gift for a far greater impact.

In our fast-paced world, the discipline of celebration is crucial. Help us slow down, savor life, and see the beauty around us—it's the nourishment our souls need today.

---

### ➔ Pray

Father, thank You for creating us with the ability to experience joy, connect with others, and honor milestones and achievements. Though it comes more naturally for me, help me cultivate the discipline of celebration, doing even more to help others recognize every blessing You've given us that we may be too busy to see right now.

---

# Day 33 Reflections:

**In what ways do you observe the gift of celebration being expressed or demonstrated in your own life?**

**When it comes to celebration, what are some barriers or obstacles your family or team struggles with?**

**How can celebration be integrated into your community, family, or workplace to foster a sense of connection, unity, and appreciation?**

> **➜ Respond**
>
> Create a yearly custom, tradition, or travel excursion that fosters a greater culture of celebration.

# Expressive Worship

*Clap your hands, all peoples! Shout to God with loud songs of joy!*

—Psalm 47:1

---

NEW EXPRESSIONS OF WORSHIP HAVE OFTEN FACED resistance throughout church history. In the 200s, people were suspicious of using any instruments in church because they were associated with debauchery and immorality, and by the 800s almost all churches were still chanting without any instruments. In the 1200s, France introduced harmonies into worship, though some people thought they were too sexual. Organs finally became commonplace by the 1400s, but the soon-to-be-created Reformed church expressed much opposition to it (which is ironic because the organ is the only instrument allowed in some Reformed churches today).[2]

> Why should the devil have all the best music?
>
> —William Booth, founder of The Salvation Army[1]

In the 1800s, William Booth, founder of The Salvation Army, incorporated rousing melodies

---

1 Andrew Wilson-Dickson, *The Story of Christian Music: From Gregorian Chant to Black Gospel: An Authoritative Illustrated Guide to All the Major Traditions in Music* (Minneapolis, MN: First Fortress Press, 2003), 139.

2 Elmer Towns, Ed Stetzer, *Perimeters of Light: Discerning Biblical Boundaries for the Emerging Church.* Shippensburg, PA: Destiny Image, Inc., 2018. Kindle. Location 1118-1196.

in his churches, garnering criticism for using worship songs that sounded like (gasp!) secular music. Booth replied, "Why should the devil have all the best music?"[3]

As you can see, throughout church history, new expressions of worship (probably introduced by Sevens) have often faced criticism for being excessive, judgment which extends to how we engage our bodies in worship as well. One incident from my early days in campus ministry comes back to me: During a meeting, a tall student in front of me raised his hands in worship, unintentionally obstructing my view of the projection screen. Frustrated, I muttered angrily "Get a prayer closet." I couldn't believe this charismatic guy was interfering with my preferred style. The audacity!

Little did I know, the Bible actually encourages the use of our bodies in worship, as reflected in various passages: Psalm 47:1 calls for the act of clapping hands, inviting all people to participate. Psalm 95:6 prompts us to bow down in worship, humbling ourselves before the Lord. Psalm 134:2 encourages lifting up our hands in praise while Psalm 33:1 exhorts us to shout for joy. Lastly, Psalm 149:3 invites us to praise His name with the joyous expression of dancing. These verses collectively emphasize the vibrant and physical nature of worship, urging us to engage our entire being in adoration.

> Expressive worship is not excessive worship.

In light of those passages, Pastor Andrew Wilson, in his book *Spirit and Sacrament*, tries to rock the boat by saying, "Given the explicit instructions of the Psalms … it is even worth asking whether churches that never play loud music, sing new songs, clap, raise hands, shout, or dance are not just reserved or conservative but actually unbiblical."[4]

As Wilson provocatively points out, biblical aspects of worship are often missing in our Western church experience. My Black and Latino friends say this is particularly hard for them, and when I merged our predominantly white

---

3   Wilson-Dickson, *The Story of Christian Music*, 139.

4   Andrew Wilson, *Spirit and Sacrament: An Invitation to Eucharismatic Worship* (Grand Rapids, MI: Zondervan, 2019), 53.

congregation with a multiethnic church, we had a few white people leave because the new preaching style and worship felt inauthentic to them. And while no one should be forced to approach God in a way that is untrue to who they are, what they characterized as excessive was actually just a more fully-formed worship expression informed by the Psalms and a reflection of communities with very different cultural histories than theirs. The Bible is clear: *Expressive worship is not excessive worship*.

***The Good News for Enthusiasts*** is that the Psalms do not just affirm your expressive style of worship, but command it. Clapping, bowing, lifting hands, shouting, and dancing are not mere suggestions but acts of obedience. After all, why should our gyms get the best use of our bodies? Why should our athletic venues be filled with our loudest claps and shouting? Is not the God who created our bodies worthy of getting our very best?

I'll never forget the time my friend Tim took me to Times Square Church in New York City. I vividly remember being in awe of the atmosphere and envious that Tim could worship so freely next to me. Having been a part of the "frozen chosen" for so long, I felt enslaved in that moment—I wanted so badly to lift my hands but felt paralyzed. Fast forward to today and now I'm "washing windows" with my hands on Sunday. I'm finally *free* and have to thank friends like Tim for showing me what true worship looks like. Though it may feel lonely at times, don't stop being you. You are inspiring the people sitting next to you even if you don't know it.

---

### → Pray

Father, help Your church embrace the vibrant expressions encouraged in the Psalms: clapping, bowing, lifting hands, shouting, and dancing. Break our fear and inhibition, freeing us to worship with our whole being. Even in moments when I feel isolated or misunderstood in my worship expressions, remind me of the impact I have on others.

---

# Day 34 Reflections:

**Share a personal experience when you felt the freedom to express your worship style authentically. How did it impact your spiritual connection with God?**

**In your experience, have you ever witnessed a clash of worship styles or expressions within your church? How did that influence the unity or diversity of worship?**

**How can you create a space where everyone feels comfortable to worship in their own unique way, regardless of cultural backgrounds or personal preferences?**

---

### → Respond

Visit a worship gathering from a different cultural background or liturgical style. Attend with an open heart and mind, observing and participating in their unique worship style. Take note of the elements that resonate with you and those that challenge you.

# Rebel with a Cause

*Be subject for the Lord's sake to every human institution, whether*

*it be to the emperor as supreme, or to governors as sent by him to*

*punish those who do evil and to praise those who do good.*

—1 Peter 2:13-14

---

GALILEO GALILEI, THE EMINENT ASTRONOMER AND PHYSICIST of the seventeenth century, was a man who embodied the essence of rebellion in a truly remarkable manner. In an era when the established order dictated that Earth stood at the center of the universe, Galileo fearlessly embraced the Copernican theory that the planets, including ours, revolve instead around the *sun*. His audacious pursuit of scientific truth challenged not only the revered teachings of Aristotle but also the authority of the Catholic Church,

> All truths are easy to understand once they are discovered; the point is to discover them.
>
> —Galileo[1]

---

1    Sam Walters, "Yes, Galileo Actually Said That," *Discover Magazine*, February 20, 2023, https://www. discovermagazine.com/the-sciences/yes-galileo-actually-said-that.

and the commitment to his beliefs ultimately led to his conviction of heresy and subsequent house arrest by the Church.[2]

Galileo exhibited many Enthusiast themes in his life, such as an insatiable curiosity about the natural world—innovative thinking that led to groundbreaking scientific contributions while still harmonizing with Scripture—and displayed an optimism in the face of opposition and adversity. Every Seven can find inspiration in a leader who forever altered our understanding of the Universe by defying the limitations imposed upon him by the powers that be out of a deep commitment to intellectual freedom.

All Sevens embody *chutzpah*, a Yiddish word describing audacity, boldness, quick-wittedness, cleverness, boundary-pushing, and courage to say

> Jesus was indeed a rebel.

or do something unconventional or unexpected.[3] Rosa Parks, during the Civil Rights movement, had *chutzpah* when she refused to give up her seat on the bus. The patriarch Abraham had *chutzpah* when he argued with God over His plans to destroy Sodom and Gomorrah. Jacob had *chutzpah* when he wrestled with God down at the Jabbok River until God blessed him. David had *chutzpah* when he went up against Goliath. They were all rebels *with* a cause.

However, when Sevens are unhealthy, they become rebellious *without* good cause—becoming rude, opinionated, dogmatic, critical, and argumentative. They channel their natural assertiveness toward getting what they want and wearing down others with their preternatural debate skills, even if they are much younger or know less about a certain topic.

When arguments lead to conflict, unlike Eights who confront it head on, Sevens choose a softer form of rebelliousness because they dislike the unpleasant feelings it stirs up. This type of implicit rebelliousness manifests as caustic humor, biting sarcasm, charm, or intellectual manipulation, more covert strategies that prevent attracting more attention and confrontation from the authorities.[4] Sevens try to

---

2  Biography.com Editors, "Galileo Biography," The Biography.com website, April 3, 2014, https://www.biography.com/scientists/galileo.

3  "Do You Have Chutzpah?," Wonderopolis, accessed June 12, 2023, https://wonderopolis.org/wonder/do-you-have-chutzpah.

4  Chestnut, *The Complete Enneagram*.

redefine authority by flattening it and making everyone equal so that there are no rules or organization limits placed on them. They say to themselves, *Someone who's on the same level as me can't tell me what to do!* But as Sevens can become relentlessly stubborn and undebatable, they usually have to learn life lessons the hard way—through painful trial and error.

The apostle Peter's words from our passage today about submission to authority may seem counterintuitive or restrictive to your independent nature. However, submitting to human authorities is not about blindly following oppressive or unjust commands. Instead, it is an act of acknowledging the order and structure God has established for our well-being and society's flourishing. By willingly placing ourselves under authority, we demonstrate respect for God's divine order and our trust in His sovereignty.

It's essential for you to discern between healthy rebellion and that which hinders your spiritual growth. Healthy rebellion challenges societal norms and oppressive structures, seeking justice and righteousness. However, rebellion that stems from a refusal to submit is often about your own restlessness and dissatisfaction, and it will hinder your relationship with God and others.

***The Good News For Enthusiasts*** is that Jesus was indeed a rebel. He fearlessly challenged oppressive religious systems and societal norms, shining a light on their injustices with love and compassion. Jesus defied legalism and self-righteousness, advocating instead for justice, mercy, and inclusivity. However, His rebellion was not driven by a desire for personal freedom but by a radical love for others, seeking their transformation and liberation. As someone created in the image of Christ, boldly embrace your chutzpah, continuing to fight for the freedom and well-being of others, just as Jesus did.

---

### ➜ Pray

Father, I am grateful for the vibrant spirit You have given me. Help me discern between healthy rebellion and rebellion that hinders my growth. Teach me to willingly submit to Your authority, trusting in Your perfect plan for my life. Fill me with the joy and freedom that comes from surrendering to You.

# Day 35 Reflections:

When in your life have you displayed *chutzpah* to challenge unjust systems or advocate for justice?

What pitfalls have you experienced as a result of unhealthy rebellion, such as being rude, opinionated, or argumentative? How can you channel your assertiveness in a more constructive and respectful manner?

How does Jesus inspire you to rebel for the sake of others? How can you embody His radical love in your interactions with authority and in fighting for the freedom and well-being of others?

## → Respond

Volunteer for a local organization that addresses social issues, speak up against injustice in conversations or on social media platforms, or support a cause that aligns with the values of love, compassion, and inclusivity.

# Be a Sponge

*Know this, my beloved brothers: let every person be*

*quick to hear, slow to speak, slow to anger.*

—James 1:19

I LOVE BOUNCING MY TWO SONS ON the trampoline, and when I time it just right, I can send my sixty-pound nine-year-old soaring toward the moon, filling him with a mix of terror and joy. As an Enthusiast, you have a similar effect on me: your lively storytelling and affirming words lift my spirits when I'm feeling low, helping me bounce back from setbacks and providing a safe landing place when I need it. You are a natural trampoline for others, propelling us to reach greater heights than we could on our own.

> The best ministry you might do today is to listen to someone's pain all the way to the bottom.
>
> —David Mathis[1]

However, as a spiritual leader, it's important not only to elevate others like a trampoline but also to listen like a sponge. You must humbly recognize that you don't possess all the answers or insights; instead, you must come

---

1   David Matthis, "Six Lessons in Good Listening," Desiring God, April 3, 2014, https://www.desiringgod.org/articles/six-lessons-in-good-listening.

to others thirsty for their wisdom and perspectives. Like a waterlogged sponge, your mind may become too saturated with your own ideas and thoughts—it's not hard for Sevens to formulate a quick response or think of three stories to share before the other person even finishes a sentence!

That is why fellow Seven and Enneagram author Sarajane Case emphasizes the need to practice selflessness in your communication: "It doesn't matter how good your story is; if you haven't expressed interest in their thoughts, they don't want to hear it. Type Sevens spend a lot of time doing things, thinking about those things, and engaging with people. This can create a buildup of untold stories. Interesting experiences, thoughts, or conversations can crowd your mind, waiting for the right time to be told. However, sometimes these stories get shared in lieu of true connection with other people. Conversations can feel like story time, leaving those engaging with you feeling like they received a good performance but not so much a great interaction."[2]

The apostle James' instruction to "be quick to hear" reveals that a truly skilled conversationalist demonstrates humility by creating space for others to share, shifting the spotlight away from themselves, showing genuine interest in others' perspectives, and being mindful of speaking out of turn. His follow-up instruction to be "slow to speak" cautions against hasty or impulsive words that can lead to misunderstandings or hurtful conversations.[3] It encourages thoughtful and considerate speech, taking time to weigh our words and respond with wisdom and grace.

As a sponge, you must squeeze out distractions so you can soak in the stories of others. This may involve silencing your phone or finding a less-distracting space to engage in conversation, and it definitely involves silencing that restless voice inside your head, urging you to "move on" when others start talking about their feelings or topics that are mundane to you. At that moment, tell yourself to slow down and hold tight. Don't try to get out of a serious conversation by telling a

---

2   Case, *The Honest Enneagram*, 177-178.

3   James 1:19

joke, reframing it into something positive, or escaping to another room when a loved one wants to work something out.

When you do speak, say what you want to say, but bring others with you, pausing along the way to ask questions so you don't take over the conversation. Don't let your excitement cause you to run ahead of them, and keep an eye on your intensity level so that it doesn't cause others to shrink back rather than lean in.

***The Good News for Enthusiasts*** is the Holy Spirit enables you to exercise self-control and demonstrate genuine care for others.[4] As you embrace the role of trampoline and sponge, let humility guide your interactions, reminding you to hold space for others, listen wholeheartedly, and resist the temptation to dominate conversations. Through your attentive listening and compassionate presence, you not only validate the worth of those you encounter but also reflect the heart of Christ, who listens to you with boundless love and grace.

---

### → Pray

Father, teach me to be a humble listener who is selfless in my communication, turning the spotlight away from me and creating space for others to share. Help me resist the temptation to rush ahead or dominate the dialogue but to bring others along and ask thoughtful questions instead. May my interactions reflect Your heart of love.

---

4   Galatians 5:22-23

# Day 36 Reflections:

**In what ways have you noticed yourself serving as a trampoline, offering support, helping people rebound from setbacks, providing a safe place to land, and empowering them to reach greater heights?**

**When have you experienced a conversation where you felt like the other person was more focused on themselves than connecting with you on a deeper level? How did that make you feel?**

**How can you intentionally create more space for others to share their stories and perspectives, making them feel heard and valued?**

---

### ➜ Respond

In the middle of your next conversation, resist the urge to interrupt and instead say, "Tell me more" to draw out their thoughts and feelings further.

# The Best Is Now

*Not that I am speaking of being in need, for I have learned in whatever*

*situation I am to be content. I know how to be brought low, and I*

*know how to abound. In any and every circumstance, I have learned*

*the secret of facing plenty and hunger, abundance and need.*

—Philippians 4:11-12

---

ON MUSICAL LEGEND FRANK SINATRA'S TOMBSTONE THE inscription reads, "The Best is Yet to Come." This popular phrase and title of his 1964 chart-topping hit[2] is also found on countless church signs, and embodies the belief that the most fulfilling and enjoyable moments are *yet* to be experienced. Can I get an Amen?

Well, hold on for a second. While this powerful saying inspires us to dream

> Why do I have three Super Bowl rings, and still think there's something greater out there for me?
>
> –Tom Brady[1]

---

1    Dave Ferguson and Jon Ferguson, *Finding Your Way Back to God: Five Awakenings to Your New Life* (Colorado Springs, CO: Multnomah Books, 2015), 41.

2    Funeral Guide, "Beautiful Epitaphs: 10 Headstone Quotes on Famous Graves," Funeral Guide, April 12, 2017, https://www.funeralguide.com/blog/beautiful-epitaphs.

about the possibilities that lie ahead, when overstated, it can lead to profound discontentment. If you constantly feed the notion that "the best is yet to come," you may unintentionally foster a culture that is never satisfied with the present reality. Enthusiasts are often guilty of attaching conditions to their happiness: "I'll be happy when …"

So, let's put things into perspective. The truth of today is the future of yesterday, which means that the longed-for "best" is happening *right now*. Think about it. One year ago, you were likely anticipating how wonderful today would be. So, rather than thinking of next year's happiness, enjoy this one!

Sevens need to redefine their idea of fun from constantly seeking "more tomorrow" to truly savoring and enjoying what they have in the present. They often resemble Tarzan, gracefully swinging from tree to tree in a vibrant jungle, moving from one desire to the next: "I want to live on the beach in LA, but I also want to live in the mountains in Colorado. Oh, and I also want to have a downtown condo in NYC!"

> The truth is today is the future of yesterday, which means that the longed-for "best" is happening right now.

Much like Tarzan forgets to stop and immerse himself in the beauty (or danger) of the jungle below, Sevens often skim the surface of life's experiences without fully embracing them. The captivating landscapes, subtle details, and serene moments often slip by unnoticed as Sevens constantly reach for the next thrilling adventure. Yet, they can discover a profound sense of fulfillment and connection with the world around them beneath the treetops in the tranquility and gratitude of the present.

Enneagram author Drew Moser aptly says, "Sevens desire contentment but often settle for excitement."[3] Essentially, deep within, Sevens yearn for a profound satisfaction, but a lack of trust in God's care for them leads to getting stuck in a cycle of planning and looking ahead, always seeking the next vine to swing from. Unfortunately, this constant mental activity disconnects them from the

---

3   Moser, *The Enneagram of Discernment*, 348.

present moment, hindering their ability to find contentment with what is right in front of them.[4]

When Tarzan the Enthusiast moves on his growth path to a Type Five and slows down to investigate what's happening down below the treeline, he can observe the delicate wildflowers that paint the forest floor, listen to the melodious songs of the birds, smell the scent of the earth and moss, and listen to the streams cascading over rocks.

This present-centered approach has immediate salience for me: rather than fantasizing about the future release of this book and its impact in a few months' time, I'm relishing the present moment. Currently, I'm immersed in the delightful tunes of the Vitamin String Quartet playing through my headphones. This devotion has occupied my thoughts all day and even enhanced my grocery shopping experience. With a newfound sense of calm, I leisurely strolled through Aldi, gathering items I knew would bring immense joy to my children when I returned. It's truly remarkable how changing our perspective can lead to amazing outcomes. This reminds me of the apostle Paul's words: "Rejoice always, pray without ceasing, give thanks in all circumstances; for this is the will of God in Christ Jesus for you."[5] The prefix "re-" denotes repetition, emphasizing Paul's command to continuously find joy in what we have today.

***The Good News for Enthusiasts*** is Paul says it's possible to be content *today* because contentment doesn't depend on the future but on the One who is with you today. In the presence of Christ, all our ordinary experiences become extraordinary. Eating a bagel, cleaning your room, or going grocery shopping can be a fulfilling experience when you do it with awe and wonder, believing the best is right now.

---

4   Riso and Hudson, *Personality Types*, 268-269.

5   1 Thessalonians 5:16-18

## → Pray

Father, help me find contentment in the present moment and appreciate the beauty around me. Guide me to trust in Your provision and let go of my constant striving for more. Fill me with joy and gratitude for what I have today. May I experience the extraordinary in the ordinary with awe and wonder through the strength Jesus gives me every day.

# Day 37 Reflections:

**How do you define contentment? What factors or circumstances do you tend to associate with being content?**

**Reflect on a time when you felt truly content. What were the contributing factors? How can you cultivate those elements in your life more consistently?**

**Consider a few of the everyday tasks you have scheduled for this week. How can you infuse them with a touch of extraordinary?**

## → Respond

Practice gratitude journaling. Set aside a few minutes each day to write down what you are grateful for. These can be small or significant, ranging from moments of joy, supportive relationships, personal accomplishments, or even the beauty of nature.

# Turning Dreams into Reality

*Look carefully then how you walk, not as unwise but as wise,*

*making the best use of the time, because the days are evil. Therefore*

*do not be foolish, but understand what the will of the Lord is.*

—Ephesians 5:15-17

---

HAVE YOU EVER BEEN CAUGHT DAYDREAMING? I get caught so often that my son jokingly asks me, "Did you go to 'Ty-land' again?" In grade school, I daydreamed so much my teacher worried I had hearing problems. After a school-mandated trip to the ear doctor, my teacher was surprised to learn my hearing was quite excellent after all.

> Dreams can become a reality when we possess a vision and a commitment to pursue them.
>
> –Walt Disney

The world needs dreamers—people like you who aren't afraid to go all in on their hopes. In 1901, a young boy named Walter was born on the northwest side of Chicago. Walter grew up spending most days "in his own head," often putting his dreams into pictures. He took his first job as a commercial illustrator at the age of eighteen and went on to become perhaps the most famous animator, voice actor, and film producer ever. "Walt" Disney pioneered the American animation industry and won a record twenty-two Oscars. His imagination was the springboard for the most popular amusement park in the world and one of the most dominant businesses in history.[1]

Many Enthusiasts describe having a Disney-like imagination, so much so that what they dream about often seems more *real* than what is actually happening! Because your imagination is so rich with awe and wonder, it's not hard to see why you might prefer living in your imagination to living in reality. Dreaming is more advantageous than *doing* when you realize you can experience all the highs in your head while avoiding all the hard work with your hands.

The average Enthusiast, especially the one-to-one subtype, easily gets stuck in their utopian visions so much that they may lose touch with what's real. Dr. Jerry Wagner reminds Sevens that "the map is not the territory," meaning our subjective representations or models of reality (the map) are not the same as the actual reality or experience itself (the territory). Wagner explains, "Our ideas reach their full reality when they are expressed and executed in the present. You can elaborate on blueprints for a house indefinitely and still not have a roof over your head. You have to build the house brick by brick, moment by moment in the here and now."[2]

Because God has given you a rich imagination for a reason, this gift must be stewarded. Though it's more pleasurable to spend time dreaming about writing that film or novel, the work required to develop the real skills to pull it off takes time, with feet planted in reality, and a dogged determination to follow through. Remember, our fantasies only become fruitful when we bring them into everyday life. You have the ability, like Walt, to create magic amid the everyday for people, but you must remember your legacy will not be determined by what you *dream* but by what you *do*—and you have a limited amount of time to do it.

---

1  Biography.com Editors, "Walt Disney Biography," Biography.com, April 3, 2014, https://www.biography.com/business-leaders/walt-disney.

2  Wagner, *Nine Lenses on the World*, 379.

Time is a resource we are forced to spend whether we want to or not; as you read this, you are "spending time." This is why the apostle Paul admonished the Ephesian Christians to make the best use of their time, reminding the young congregation that the "days are evil."[3] Unhealthy Sevens are guilty, along with many Christians, of being so heavenly minded they do no earthly good. But your life can tell a different story.

***The Good News for Enthusiasts*** is dreamers aren't expected to change the world on their own—they have doers to come alongside. Although Walt Disney was perceived to be a Type A leader, those who knew him said he was shy, self-deprecating, and insecure about his abilities. Walt was able to accomplish so much largely because of an older, business-savvy brother, Roy, who helped turn Walt's dream into reality.[4]

As a dreamer, you must look around to see who God has provided to turn your dreams into reality— friends who can help you when you start feeling small, inadequate, disheartened, or paralyzed. Your potential for changing the world will likely not be limited by your dreams but by whether or not you partner with others who can help bring those God-given dreams to fruition here and now.

---

### → Pray

Father, thank You for the gift of imagination and the ability to dream. Help me not to get lost in my dreams but to take action in the present. Give me wisdom to use my time wisely and the courage to turn my dreams into reality. Guide me to find the right people who can support and help me bring my dreams to fruition.

---

3  Ephesians 5:16

4  "Walt Disney Biography," https://www.biography.com/business-leaders/walt-disney.

# Day 38 Reflections:

When have you found yourself caught up in daydreaming or living in your imagination more than in reality? How has this affected your ability to take action and pursue your dreams?

How can you ensure your dreams are grounded in reality and connected to tangible actions? Who can you collaborate with to help you achieve a dream or goal?

When during the week can you create a block of time to pay the bills, get groceries, do laundry, and other must-do tasks to help you be more productive with your time and more practical for those around you?

---

### → Respond

Write down all the dreams that remain unfulfilled in your life. Courageously decide to act on one of these today or in the following week.

# Facing Your Fear

*Since therefore the children share in flesh and blood, he himself likewise*

*partook of the same things, that through death he might destroy the*

*one who has the power of death, that is, the devil, and deliver all*

*those who through fear of death were subject to lifelong slavery.*

—Hebrews 2:14-15

---

I FOUND IT VERY ODD WHEN FIRST learning the Enneagram that Sevens were in a triad along with Fives and Sixes with *fear* as the dominant emotion. I thought it must be some mistake: the Sevens I know are not anxious or scared. If they could put a verse on a coffee cup it would be, "And which of you by being anxious can add a single hour to his span of life?"[2] However, I discovered that even though Sevens may not feel actively afraid, fear still holds significant influence over them, pulling the strings behind their constant

> The joy of God has gone through the poverty of the manger and the agony of the cross; that is why it is invincible, irrefutable.
>
> –Dietrich Bonhoeffer[1]

---

1   Dietrich Bonhoeffer, *Dietrich Bonhoeffer Works, Volume 16 / Conspiracy and Imprisonment, 1940–1945* (Minneapolis, MN: Fortress Press, 2006).

2   Matthew 6:27

movement, planning, escapism, and impulsiveness. The average Seven remains unaware of this because they never pause long enough to confront it directly.

Avoiding the confrontation of fears leads to a life of perpetual enslavement, as the author of Hebrews warned. Fear will keep you running like a fugitive for the rest of your life, making you live off the fumes of excitement instead of the fuel of peace.

The greatest fear for many of us, including Sevens, is death, which we must face head-on. By conquering this giant, all other smaller fears, like boredom, become much easier to overcome. The idea of being trapped indefinitely in a grave is the ultimate dread for a Seven, representing a life without escape or fun.

Let me share the story of my friend Michelle, a vibrant Enthusiast with a contagious smile. She faced her worst fear when she received a devastating ALS (Amyotrophic Lateral Sclerosis) diagnosis. This disease gradually took away her ability to control her muscles, ultimately leading to paralysis and respiratory failure. Over the years, I witnessed Michelle become trapped within her own body by losing the ability to walk and talk, reduced to scribbling a few words on a sketch pad to communicate. She had to grieve the loss of everyday activities like cooking, doing life with her husband, and playing with her grandchildren. I saw her struggle with anxiety attacks as fluid filled her lungs, making it difficult for her to breathe. It was a truly painful and challenging journey to watch.

But Michelle, unable to escape her worst fear, made a courageous decision to face it head-on. She used her gift of realistic positivity as a Seven to overcome the hardships. As her family and friends walked into the darkness surrounding her, Michelle remained a beacon of light, ministering to us with her smile even when words failed us.

During this season, God did not abandon Michelle. Instead, He drew closer to her through His people. Michelle felt the heaviness lift when friends visited on

Sunday afternoons and prayed for her. Her daughters' tender words brought comfort, the doorbell ringing with flower deliveries lifted her spirits, and the worship team singing over her touched her heart. Her husband Dan would carry her into bed every night and hold her hand under the covers, demonstrating the Father's nearness.

***The Good News for Enthusiasts*** is Jesus removed the sting of death by putting Himself through our worst fear: He confronted death directly and emerged victorious. He did this so that we could be freed from the fear of being trapped in the grave forever. Jesus willingly endured the loss of His dignity, being stripped, mocked, spit on, and beaten so that He could clothe you with honor in your final days. Now, because the power of death has been destroyed, your pain has an expiration date—death will be "the last enemy to be destroyed."[3]

What's truly remarkable about Jesus' story is how a criminal on the cross found salvation after witnessing His suffering. Before, Jesus' words held little weight in his heart, but after witnessing Jesus' unconventional suffering, the criminal's dying heart came alive. Similarly, hundreds of people attended Michelle's funeral, sharing how their hearts were transformed after seeing Michelle's race completed, after seeing her suffer truly for the joy set before her. Your own journey of facing your fears head-on, no matter how big or small, can unlock a life of peace and inspire others. So today, with all sincerity, I encourage you to look death in the face and tell it to go to hell.

---

**→ Pray**

Father, though fear may not always be apparent, I acknowledge its influence in my constant busyness and escape. Help me slow down and turn toward my fears, for in doing so, I can find true freedom. May others witness Your transformative power in my life and be inspired to face their fears with courage and faith.

---

3   1 Corinthians 15:26

# Day 39 Reflections:

**How does Michelle's courageous story inspire and motivate you today?**

**What hidden areas of fear in your life have you not confronted because you haven't slowed down? If so, what are they?**

**What is your greatest fear? If it were to happen, what would be the best possible outcome? How does Jesus' victory over death free you from this fear?**

> **→ Respond**
>
> Create a written inventory of your fears, worries, and stressors. This simple act of clearing your mind through this technique can bring about a sense of calm and alleviate feeling overwhelmed.

# Wonderful Plans

*For I know the plans I have for you, declares the Lord, plans for*

*welfare and not for evil, to give you a future and a hope.*

—Jeremiah 29:11

---

DURING A VERY DARK TIME, THE PROPHET Jeremiah penned a letter to his fellow Israelites. They had been exiled, forcibly removed from their homeland and taken to Babylon in chains. Not only that, but it appeared that their God was telling them to get comfortable—they would be there for a while. In their suffering, uncertainty about their future, and longing to return home to Jerusalem, Jeremiah delivered a healing message about God's intentions to prosper His people, not to harm them; to give them hope, and a future.

> I don't want to earn my living; I want to live.
>
> —Oscar Wilde

Although this passage has been taken out of context many times before and applied to many different settings, what I think is universally true is that you don't have to be anxious about the future because God has wonderful plans for you—no matter how many times you fail. Psalm 139 reminds you that God created you in your mother's womb with intention and purpose, giving you unique talents, passions, and gifts. Ephesians 2:10 affirms that God has good works prepared for you. I mention these today to remind you God has so much more in store for you—He's not done with you yet.

As a Seven, one of the greatest challenges you may face is avoiding the temptation to trade *purpose for potential.* When you chase your potential, you take stock of all your inherent abilities and talents and go pursue whatever is in the realm of possibility on any given day. Chasing potential feels very promising every single time because, newsflash, Sevens are good at mostly everything! You are a jack of all trades who can literally become a news anchor, dentist, musician, pastor, or realtor. The sky's the limit and that is precisely your problem. You can be almost anything you want to be.

Therefore, the solution is to rise above your potential by discovering your purpose. In other words, you need to shift your focus from what you *could* be to who you're *meant* to be. Chasing the potential of who you could be is always fun, but discovering who you're meant to be will always be more fulfilling. Chasing your potential is fast and easy, but discovering your purpose takes dedication. Chasing potential often comes at the expense of others' well-being because the focus is on you, whereas discovering your purpose aligns you with God's redemptive plan for the world.

> One of the greatest challenges you may face is avoiding the temptation to trade purpose for potential.

As you are starting to see, the main difference between chasing potential and purpose has to do with the process. Simply put: Chasing your potential is the self-driven process of acting impulsively on fun ideas that bring about temporary pleasure or external validation from others, whereas chasing your purpose is a slow God-guided process, requires much trial-and-error, and could make you unpopular but ultimately will leave you with a joy no one can take away from you.

Start by putting your plans in God's hands. Surrender all the things you could potentially do and invite Him to direct your steps. Then reflect on the natural talents and abilities you've been affirmed for the most in your life. I always remind my Seven friends to *follow the affirmation.* Next, search for the need. Theologian Frederick Buechner says "calling" is "the place where your deep gladness and the world's deep hunger meet."[1] In other words, what are the greatest needs around you that would give you the deepest fulfillment to meet? Finally, be patient and trust God's timing. Very rarely will God reveal His plans overnight. Just ask Joseph, Moses, Hannah, David, Ruth, Job, Mary, Paul, and a host of others who *waited* on God for years to discover their purpose.

***The Good News for Enthusiasts*** is that God "is able to do far more abundantly than all that we ask or think, according to the power at work within us."[2] God's purpose for you far exceeds what you think your potential is! Whatever you think you can do, just stop and think bigger. God is more excited about the future than you and can't wait to reveal the wonderful plans He has in store.

---

### → Pray

Father, thank You for the hope and future You have promised me. Help me to rise above my potential and discover my purpose. I surrender my plans to You and invite Your direction. Show me where my deep gladness aligns with the world's deep hunger. Teach me patience as You do abundantly more than I can ask or imagine.

---

1 Frederick Buechner, *Wishful Thinking: A Theological ABC* (London, Mowbray, 1994), 119.

2 Ephesians 3:20

# Day 40 Reflections:

**When did you pursue something simply because you "could" do it but later discovered that it wasn't what you were truly "meant" to do? What did you learn from that experience?**

**Think about how your natural talents align with the needs of the world. Where do you see the greatest opportunity to make a meaningful impact and find deep fulfillment in meeting those needs?**

**What do you want to be remembered for?**

---

### → Respond

Find a life coach or spiritual mentor to come alongside and support you in accomplishing your dreams. Start working toward something today that seems impossible without God's supernatural power and grace.

FATHER, I AM DEEPLY GRATEFUL TO YOU for creating me in Your image as Your beloved child. You created me to specifically reflect Your joy and abundance. I confess that my fast pace has often left me feeling overextended and dismissed by others. I have found myself being reckless, impulsive, excessive, and unreliable at times. You, being rich in mercy, saw me from heaven and sent Your life-giving Son, Jesus, to die on the cross when I was anxious and restless. Now, I revel in the fact that You have invited me into Your presence, where I find unending joy and pleasure. Clothed with the power of the Holy Spirit, I will view freedom as an opportunity to serve others, not an excuse for self-indulgence. Putting off childish ways and putting on my new, disciplined self made in Christ's image, I will pursue reliability over impulsivity, contentment over a grass-is-greener mentality, empathy over toxic positivity, and grow into my potential by courageously confronting my pain rather than finding the quickest way around it.

# Three Types of Enthusiasts

BELOW IS A SUMMARY OF THE THREE types of Sevens (called subtypes) from the teaching of Beatrice Chestnut, whose book, *The Complete Enneagram* covers all twenty-seven subtypes of the main nine Enneagram types.[1] As discussed in the introduction, these subtypes help us drill down the different nuances of the Enthusiast.

Warning: many of these descriptions will seem overly negative. However, one of the main purposes of the Enneagram is to help us discover our "shadow self"— the ways we interact with the world unconsciously and often in times of stress. These descriptions are not indictments; rather, they are a further opportunity to deepen our awareness of how we naturally interact with the world and perhaps ways to make healthier choices for ourselves and those around us.

## The Self-Preservation Seven

The Self-Preservation Seven seeks to build strategic alliances with others or create a family network to get their needs met. Having a scarcity mindset, they must acquire food, money, and other resources to survive or else panic sets in. They are skilled networkers who know how to find the best deal and get what they want. If they don't keep their ear to the ground for new opportunities, they fear they will miss out. These Sevens tend to be more down-to-earth, practical, and materialistic than the other subtypes. When in an unhealthy state, they may adopt a "hedonistic" or "pleasure-seeking" lifestyle. This subtype tends to be more consumeristic and may turn to sex, food, drinking, or shopping to escape the difficulties of life. This subtype is the most committed, often enjoying long relationships with their partner or a group they're heavily invested in. These Sevens may look like Sixes because they are more isolated, careful, and strategic, but they are far more positive than Sixes. They may also appear like Eights because they are people-oriented and impulsive, but they tend to be motivated by a fear of survival while Eights tend to be fearless.

---

1  Chestnut, *The Complete Enneagram*.

## The One-to-One Seven

While the Self-Preservation Seven is more sly, cunning, pragmatic and not easily hypnotized, the One-to-One is more of a heavenly-minded, light-hearted, enjoyer of life who tends to be more gullible. These thrill-seekers love falling in love with wild ideas, new possibilities, and intriguing people, and they see the world through rose-colored glasses. They are dreamers with rich imaginations who are drawn to live inside the idealized world they create in their head rather than the boring, mundane, and painful real world. They have a tendency to be too (unrealistically) happy and take refuge in optimism, causing a fixation on the positives and dismissal of the negatives. Their minds move quickly, allowing them to adapt, improvise, and do many things at once. When unhealthy, they have a restless energy that may cause them to escape to crazy schemes or love affairs or try to do too much and burnout. They seek acceptance, appreciation, and recognition from others, often through charming wit and humor. Because they prefer the feelings of infatuation that occur in the early stages of a relationship, project, or job, they often have a harder time with long-term commitment.

## The Social Seven

The Social Seven is the "countertype" because they try to avoid being (or looking) excessive in their search for pleasure. They hide their desire for fun in altruistic pursuits and causes. They adopt the role of helper, seeking to serve others, alleviate pain, and take less for themselves so others can have more. They crave love and recognition, avoid conflict, and want to be seen as a good person for all their sacrifices. Desiring to have a pure character and life, they may become too puritanical about their health or spiritual life—and they look down on others who aren't pursuing these things as well. They are enthusiastic visionaries with incredible social skills who imagine a better world and are great at mobilizing people toward that end. They surround themselves with friends who share their interests and engage in stimulating conversations. Authority is seen as unnecessary and restrictive. They tend to get over-committed and often have to cancel on others. They may be confused with Twos because of their desire to be of help and service, but Sevens are in touch with their own needs whereas Twos often don't know what they need. They may also look like Fives, who make a virtue out of living on less, or like Ones, who strive to be good and pure.

# *Next Steps*

I'M SO PROUD OF YOU FOR FINISHING this 40-day journey. That's a big accomplishment! Though this book isn't small by any means, you may feel (like me) that we've only begun to explore the tip of the iceberg. You're probably wondering: *What now? My eyes have been opened, I've grown in greater self-awareness and empathy, and now I'm ready to take the next step!* Here are some ideas:

1. Follow "Gospel for Enneagram" on Instagram, YouTube, Facebook, or Twitter to continue learning and engaging.

2. Download my free resource called *Should Christians Use The Enneagram?* at gospelforenneagram.com.

3. Leave an honest review (or star rating) online or share on social media so others can find it.

4. Visit my website, gospelforenneagram.com, to find more helpful links and resources.

5. Join a church community where you can continue to grow in your knowledge of God and self. To go the distance, find a mentor, coach, or support system.

6. Ask a friend, spouse, or mentor to meet regularly with you to discuss the insights God has revealed to you through this book. Invite them, along with your small group, to get a devotional on their Enneagram type and share what they learn with you.

7. Email me with any thoughts, questions, or feedback to tyler@gospelforenneagram.com. I'd love to hear from you!

# Acknowledgements

My wife: Lindsey, you show me the gospel every day by loving me for who I am and not what I do. Thank you for your tremendous encouragement to be a writer and for bearing with my workaholic tendencies. I want to be more like you.

My editors: Joshua, thank you for bringing your incredible creativity to the table. Your re-rewrites helped elevate my writing to a whole new level. Stephanie, because you are a Two, I appreciate that you took your time through this book, offering a tremendous amount of encouragement along the way. Your helpful comments made this book so much better than what it would have been. Thank you for Lee Ann, your veteran experience and thoroughness increased the value of this book tremendously.

My coach: John Fooshee, thank you for your Enneagram coaching and partnership. I'm deeply grateful for your willingness to come alongside me and put wind in my sails.

My influences: I wouldn't have been able to pull this off without a multitude of direct and indirect influences such as pastors, teachers, and writers (including you, mom!) over the years. I'm deeply grateful for the spiritual heroes that have come before me and shaped me.

# www.GospelForEnneagram.com

Follow us:

 /GospelForEnneagram

 @GospelForEnneagram

 @GospelForGram

 Gospel For Enneagram